Cambridge First Certificate

Examination Practice 2

Self-study Edition

Louise Hashemi
*University of Cambridge
Local Examinations Syndicate*

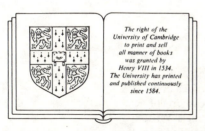

The right of the
University of Cambridge
to print and sell
all manner of books
was granted by
Henry VIII in 1534.
The University has printed
and published continuously
since 1584.

Cambridge University Press
Cambridge
New York   Port Chester
Melbourne   Sydney

Published by the Press Syndicate of the University of Cambridge
The Pitt Building, Trumpington Street, Cambridge CB2 1RP
40 West 20th Street, New York, NY 10011–4211, USA
10 Stamford Road, Oakleigh, Melbourne 3166, Australia

© Cambridge University Press 1991

First published 1991

Printed in Great Britain at the University Press, Cambridge

ISBN 0 521 38762 0 Self-study Edition
ISBN 0 521 40698 6 Cassette

GO

Cambridge First Certificate
Examination Practice 2
Self-study Edition

This book prepares you specifically for the Cambridge First Certificate Examination.

Cambridge University Press also publishes a coursebook, *Progress to First Certificate*, for which there is a *Self-study Student's Book*. This special edition includes the full text of the Student's Book as well as model answers to all the exercises, self-study notes giving advice, and tapescripts for all the listening exercises.

CAMBRIDGE
EXAMINATIONS
PUBLISHING

**Progress
to First
Certificate**

SELF-STUDY STUDENT'S BOOK

Leo Jones

...NIVERSITY PRESS

Contents

Thanks

I would like to thank Chris Jones. Much of the commentary on the multiple-choice questions in the Key comes from his software version of *Cambridge First Certificate Examination Practice 2*.

I would also like to thank Abbas for taking part in the Interview, and Alison Silver, Will Capel and Jeanne McCarten for their help in the preparation of the book.

To the student

This book is to help those of you who are preparing for the University of Cambridge First Certificate in English examination and who are working mostly or entirely on your own. It provides practice in all the five papers of the FCE and gives suggestions about how to study for the examination. The book contains four complete sets of written papers and a separate section dealing with Paper 5, the Interview.

For details of examination regulations and a list of centres where you can take FCE, write to:
University of Cambridge Local Examinations Syndicate,
1 Hills Road, Cambridge CB1 2EU, England.

Introduction

What is FCE?

We begin with a brief description of the five papers of the exam. (For more details, see Part One Study Notes on p. 8.)

PAPER 1   READING COMPREHENSION   (1 hour)

Section A consists of twenty-five multiple-choice items in the form of a sentence with a blank to be filled by one of four words or phrases.
Section B consists of fifteen multiple-choice items based on three or more reading passages of different types.
During the examination you must mark your answers on the Reading Comprehension Answer Sheet (see p. 210). The supervisor will tell you how to do this.

PAPER 2   COMPOSITION   (1½ hours)

In this paper there are five topics from which you choose two. Possible topics include a letter, a description, a narrative, a discussion and a speech. There is also a composition topic based on the optional reading. (See *Writing about the set books* on p. 11.) In this book the questions based on optional reading are set on the kind of books that are prescribed each year. These are not the books prescribed for any particular year; they are just given as examples.

PAPER 3   USE OF ENGLISH   (2 hours)

In this paper there are exercises of various kinds which test your control of English usage and grammatical structure. There is also a directed writing exercise where you study a text which normally contains an illustration, map or diagram. You have to extract the required information and present it clearly.

PAPER 4   LISTENING COMPREHENSION
(20 to 30 minutes)

Here you answer a variety of questions on recorded passages (normally three) from English broadcasts, interviews, announcements, phone messages and conversations. Each passage is heard twice. At the end, you are given five minutes to transfer your answers to the Listening Comprehension Answer Sheet (see p. 211). The supervisor will tell you how to do this.

PAPER 5   INTERVIEW   (approximately 15 minutes)

You talk to an examiner (or another candidate, see p. 197) about yourself and then about a picture which you are shown. You may be asked to comment on a short piece of writing, but you do not have to read aloud. You will also take part in a brief discussion or role play.

Working on your own

Preparing for an examination like the First Certificate on your own is not always easy, but it is certainly possible if you are prepared to work hard in a methodical way. Here are the answers to some questions you may have.

When can I enter for this exam?
First Certificate is not an elementary examination. Make sure that you have reached a reasonable standard *before* you decide to enter. If you are not sure about your standard, a good check is to try Question 1 of Paper 3 (for example, in Practice Test 1 on p. 28). If you cannot correctly fill at least one third of the gaps without using a dictionary, you are probably going to waste your money. Keep working at your English for another six months, then think again about entering. You can take the exam in December or June. Write to the address on p. 1 for details.

What do I need?
In the following two lists you will find the books and other materials you need to work effectively. Some of them are essential, others are useful but not essential.

Essential items

- A good English/English dictionary
- A reliable modern reference grammar of English
  (Make sure you get ones for *foreign* students of the language.)

- A cassette player

Useful items

- An *up-to-date* translating dictionary (English/your language)
- A radio
- A video recorder

How should I organize my studying?
Be realistic. Don't plan to do more than you can, you will only disappoint yourself.

Don't plan to give up *all* your free time to studying. Studying hard for one hour four times a week can be very effective. In fact, short sessions are probably best, because your memory won't get tired, and so you will remember what you study.

Try to study in a quiet place so that you can concentrate well.

Be organized. Write out a timetable and *follow it*. Spend a few minutes of each study period revising what you did last time.

Don't spend too much time on details! Don't look up every new word in a dictionary. Practise guessing the word by looking at the words around it (its 'context'). You can always check your guess later if you need to. This is a much better way to fix the meaning in your head.

Don't imagine that language study is only exercises and grammar books. Although these are important, the best students also spend time relaxing with English stories and magazines, getting a feeling for the way the language works. Use your leisure to help you. Find out about English language radio broadcasts you can listen to. You can write to the British Council in your country or contact the Embassies of Britain, USA, Australia and so on for information. Details of BBC overseas broadcasting are available from Bush House, PO Box 76, London WC2B 4PH, England.

If you enjoy music, try to find recordings of songs in English and listen to the words. Many cassettes and LPs have the words printed on them.

If you have a video, it should be possible to hire English language films in many places. This is even better than English language theatre or cinema, because you can replay the tape to help you check what the actors are saying.

Talk English whenever you can. For example, if you have friends studying English, arrange to speak English together once a week. Don't worry if you have few chances to meet native speakers. Remember most people learning English nowadays only use the language to communicate with other non-native speakers.

Try to find a 'penfriend': exchange letters in English with friends who may be studying English in another town, or with any English-speaking people you may know.

Using this book

Before you start work, it is necessary for you to understand how this book is organized.

PART ONE   Study Notes

In Part One each part of the test is described in detail. It explains what you have to do for each question and suggests ways of preparing yourself to give the best answers. It also suggests how you should use Part Two Practice Tests and Part Three The Key.

PART TWO   Practice Tests

In Part Two there are four sets of examination papers for Reading Comprehension, Composition, Use of English and Listening Comprehension. (For the Interview, see Part Four below.)

PART THREE   The Key

In Part Three you are given the *answers* to the Practice Tests. Part Three also contains sample plans for all the compositions (except for compositions on the set books, see p. 11). For Paper 1 Reading Comprehension, wrong answers are explained as well.

   The Key does not give meanings of words, because you can find these in your dictionary, but it does help you to understand how words are used.

PART FOUR   The Interview

This book offers you:
- information about the oral (p. 197)
- a sample Interview on the cassette (Tapescript p. 202)
- a commentary on the recorded sample Interview, giving useful suggestions (see Tapescript)

These will help you to get a good idea of what the Interview is like, and to plan your preparation.

Now you are ready to start reading Part One.

PART ONE   Study Notes

PAPER 1   READING COMPREHENSION

SECTION A

Questions 1–25   Filling gaps in sentences

1 It's a good idea to see your doctor regularly for ....
   A a revision   B a control   C an investigation   D a check-up

2 I lost too much money betting at the races last time, so you won't ....
   me to go again.
   A convince   B impress   C persuade   D urge

WHAT DOES IT TEST?

Section A may be testing your knowledge of vocabulary, grammar, or how
much you know about the way words can be used (for example, we can say
'This jacket is too small for me' but not, 'This jacket is too little for me'). It also
tests phrasal verbs, prepositions and connectors.

SUGGESTED METHOD OF WORKING

1 Read the sentence and try to understand the whole meaning.
2 Think about what you would put in the gap.
3 Look at the four words and see which is best. The sentence contains clues
   which should help you to decide.
For example, in the question shown above the correct answer is 'a check-up'
because this is the word we use when we go to the doctor to make sure we are
healthy.

When you have finished the sentences in each practice test, look at the Key in
Part Three. Here you will find the correct answers. You will also find example
sentences for the other three words (called the *distractors*) to help you

understand why they are not correct for that sentence. You can see how the
distractors should be used.

**It is important to realize that the notes give examples of usage, not meanings.
This is because you can look up meanings in your dictionary.**

SECTION B

Questions 26–40   Multiple-choice reading comprehension passages

~~ademic po~~   ~~,~~ five y   three y   ~~be~~ ~~he patte~~
Granny Ollerenshaw, in the cottage, had been immovable, unchanged and
unchanging. They called it Eel Cottage: over the doorway there was a square sign
which announced EEL 1779. For years Frances had thought that this meant the
fish which lived in muddy ditches; only later, looking more closely, did she
realize that the mysterious word must have been the builder's or owner's
initials. The cottage was a basic cottage, the kind that small children draw: low,
a door in the middle, two windows downstairs, two windows upstairs. It was
built of red brick, the brick of the district, with a red-tiled steep roof.

26   Why didn't Frances remember very much about Tockley?
    A   There was nothing special in the town.
    B   She had only been there once or twice.
    C   She had been abroad for a long time.
    D   The town had changed a great deal since her childhood.

WHAT DOES IT TEST?

This section tests your understanding of short passages of English. Some of the
questions test your understanding of a small part of the passage, some of them
test your understanding of its general meaning. For each of the three or four
passages, there are several questions, with four possible answers. Only one
answer is correct. Have a quick look at pp. 21–26 and then come back to this
page. You may have noticed that the questions may be either a real question,
like number 26, or you may have to choose the best ending for a sentence, like
number 31.

SUGGESTED METHOD FOR EACH PASSAGE

There are different ways of doing these questions. Some people prefer the 'Step-by-step' method, others prefer the 'Signposts' method.

Step-by-step

Advantage: Very thorough
Disadvantage: Takes more time

1   Read the passage through very quickly, just to get a general idea of what it is about.
2   Read the questions.
3   *Either*
    Ignore the answers at this stage. Try to decide on the answer by looking at the passage again – carefully this time – then choosing the answer which fits your idea.
    or
    Read all the possible answers, then study the passage and decide which is best.

Signposts

Advantage: Quick
Disadvantage: The distractors may put wrong ideas into your head and confuse you

1   Read through the questions and answers. Use them as 'signposts' to help you find out what you need to learn from the passage.
2   Study the passage and decide which is the best answer for each question.

Try working in different ways to see which suits you best.

USING THE KEY

Check your answers using the Key and your dictionary if necessary. You will find explanations about incorrect answers as well as correct ones. Read these carefully, as they will help you to understand how multiple-choice questions work.

PAPER 2   COMPOSITION

WHAT DOES IT TEST?

This paper tests your ability to communicate your ideas in written English, using well-organized, clear, accurate and appropriate language. You are expected to write two compositions, each between 120 and 180 words long. They will normally be divided into between two and five short paragraphs.

You will need to practise all sorts of compositions, but first you must learn to identify the different types. These are:

Narrative, or telling a story. Any composition title which asks you 'What happened?', for example, composition number 3 on p. 27.

Discussion. A composition which asks for your opinion or feelings about a subject, for example, composition number 4 on p. 27.

Description, or information. A composition title which asks you 'What is X like?', for example, composition number 1 on p. 27.

Letters. These may really be one of the types of composition mentioned above. They may be formal or informal. You may also be asked to explain, complain, apologize etc., for example, composition number 1 on p. 27.

Speeches. These too are often a different way of asking you to describe, narrate or say what you feel. You are expected to write as if you were speaking to a group of people, for example, composition number 2 on p. 27.

Writing about the set books
It is not essential to read these books as there is only one question on them in this paper. However, there are two reasons why preparing at least one of the books can be a good idea. First, this gives you an extra choice of composition. Second, it allows you to be sure that there will be at least one subject which you know something about, so you do not have to spend a lot of time searching for ideas.

You do not need to study special techniques for answering the composition questions on the set books. The examiner who marks your paper will be interested in how well you can use your English. She is not really concerned about how original your ideas are. Actually these questions are very similar to the other questions on Paper 2. For example, you have to explain what happened, or why it happened, or give your opinion of events or people. You should plan these compositions just as you would any others.

This book does not give special notes about the set book questions because the titles change very frequently. The examples given allow you to see what *sort* of questions you might be asked. Information about set books is in the UCLES Regulations (see p. 1).

SUGGESTED METHOD OF WORKING

There is a Checklist and Sample Plan for each of the composition titles in Part
Three of this book (except for those on set books, for which, see above).

First attempts
At first, you should use the Checklist and Sample Plan in Part Three to help you
before you begin planning.

General practice
After you have done several compositions, try working through the planning
stage, then checking in Part Three to see whether you have missed anything
important before you begin to write the composition.

Examination practice
Lastly, try making your plan and writing your composition just as if you were in
the examination room. Look at Part Three after you have finished in order to
help you check your work.

Of course, your ideas will not always be the same as the ones in the Sample
Plans, but you should think things through in the same way.

What is in the Checklist?

Task Check
Go through the question word by word to make sure you understand what you
have to do. Note down the main ideas you must mention.

Register Check
Think about the style and tone you must use. This depends on what you are
writing about and who your reader is supposed to be.
Examples:
– Will you write in the same way if you are writing a letter to your best friend,
  or a letter applying for a job?
– Will you use the same style to tell an exciting story, or to give your opinion
  about a serious social issue?
The answers must be 'No'.

In what ways will your compositions be different? The best way to learn about
register in English is to read as many different things as you can. Look out for
verb forms (when do you find 'won't' and when do you find 'will not'?). When
can you use slang expressions? How do you begin and end different types of
letters?

Technique
This is when you work out the best approach to the task set. Do you need to think up lots of ideas and then organize them? Try brainstorming (see for example p. 182).

Do you know the story you are going to tell, but need to decide the order in which you will present the events? Try writing a 'skeleton' in note form, then put it into numbered paragraphs before you start to write (see for example p. 180).

Do you need to remember facts and then sort them into areas? Try making a list, then grouping them into paragraphs (see for example p. 180).

DANGER! Before starting to plan in detail, think whether you have written anything like this before. Did you make any mistakes which you must take care to avoid? In this book, the DANGER! notes show how students may make serious errors.

What is in a Sample Plan?

There are usually two or three stages in planning well:

1   Ideas – making rough notes of what you want to write about. This may be a brainstorm, or a list, or a skeleton story.
2   Organization – deciding the order in which you will present your ideas and dividing them into paragraphs.
3   Words – thinking about the language you will need. If you don't know the exact word for something, find others that will describe it.

It can also be helpful if you think of any good expressions or idioms that you know that would fit into the composition you are planning (for example, see p. 104).

DOING A 'MOCK'

This is when you do a whole paper, just as if you were in the examination. It is best to prepare gradually, by writing lots of individual compositions under examination conditions, before trying to do a whole paper. As well as practising the routine described above, you need to get used to working without reference books and in a limited time.

Have your watch or a clock where you can see it. You may even decide to set the alarm!

For a whole paper your timing should be something like this:

Minutes

0 – 5	Read through the questions and decide which two you will answer.
6 – 15	Plan the first composition.
16 – 36	Write it.
37 – 45	Check it.
46 – 55	Plan the second one.
56 – 76	Write it.
77 – 85	Check it.
86 – 90	Final check.

This is good because:
– It allows you to write an average of ten words per minute, which is quite easy if you have planned properly and know what you want to say.
– It also allows plenty of time to check your spelling and grammar, and builds in a space at the end in case you suddenly realize that you have missed out something important.

PAPER 3   USE OF ENGLISH

WHAT DOES IT TEST?

This paper tests your ability to use English accurately, so you must pay special attention to your grammar, spelling and punctuation. The questions are described in detail below.

WORKING THROUGH PAPER 3

First attempt
Work through Practice Test 1 Paper 3 question by question, looking at the notes on each question below and the answers in the Key as you work. This will help you to understand how to approach this paper.

General practice
Do Paper 3 of the other tests under examination conditions, leaving your checking until the end.

QUESTION 1

WHAT DOES IT TEST?

Carter was usually able to catch the 6.35 train from Euston. This brought
..........ticket..........(1) to the town where he lived at 7.12. His bicycle waited
..........for..........(2) him at the station – the ticket-collector always looked
..........after..........(3) it for him. Then he ....reached..........(4) home, changing his
route from day to day. He crossed the canal ....and..........(5), turned
..........round..........(6) the church and up the hill to his small semi-detached

This question, called a 'Modified Cloze Test', has a short passage with twenty
gaps in it. You must fill each gap with *ONE* word only. These are often verbs,
prepositions or linking words of some sort, testing your knowledge of how the
language is structured.

SUGGESTED METHOD OF WORKING

1   Read the whole passage through, ignoring the gaps, and try to understand
    the general meaning as well as you can.
2   Think about each gap in turn. You should think about three things:
    a) the words immediately before the gap
    b) the words immediately after the gap
    c) how the gap is related to the structure of other parts of the passage – this
       may influence the tense used, for example, Practice Test 1 Paper 3
       Question 1 (20), p. 28.
3   If you are 'stuck', go on to the next gap. Sometimes the difficult ones
    become easier when the passage is more or less complete.
4   Check your answers. Make sure that you have not put plural verbs with
    singular subjects, and so on. Do not leave any gaps unfilled. A hopeful
    guess might be right, but an empty space has no chance of a mark!

QUESTION 2

WHAT DOES IT TEST?

a) 'Why don't you put a better lock on the door, Barry?' said John.

   John suggested ....

b) Although both his legs were broken in the crash, he managed to get out of the car before it exploded.

   Despite his ....

This is called 'sentence transformation'. You are given a series of sentences which you must re-write without changing the meaning. This tests your knowledge of grammar and usage. The sort of structures tested are: active/ passive verbs; direct/indirect speech; gerund/infinitive structures after certain words and phrases; participles; relative clauses; comparatives and superlatives.

Sometimes there may be more than one correct way of answering. The Key at the back of this book will help you to understand what is required.

SUGGESTED METHOD OF WORKING

Try to decide what the examiner is looking for. Don't be afraid to use part of the original sentence in your new one. Make sure your transformed sentence really means the same as the original. Check your punctuation, especially apostrophes and direct speech marks.

QUESTIONS 3, 4 and 5

WHAT DO THEY TEST?

These are the ones which are most likely to change from year to year, so be especially careful to read the instructions for each question very thoroughly. Question 3 often tests the vocabulary of a particular subject, such as money or music. You are not expected to know any specialist jargon, of course. Question 4 often tests the meaning of similar words, for example, a group of phrasal verbs.

Question 5 usually involves writing sentences, either filling gaps in a conversation or expanding sets of words to construct a letter.

SUGGESTED METHOD OF WORKING

These questions do vary, so be sure to look at the example closely before starting each question.

QUESTION 6

WHAT DOES IT TEST?

This is a question designed to test your ability to understand what you read and then present it in a different form.

SUGGESTED METHOD OF WORKING

Read the instructions very carefully, and look at all the information you are given. Do not be afraid to mark the text by underlining or highlighting, if this helps you to sort out the information you need. It may also help to make brief notes before you start to write your answers. The Key in Part Three of this book shows you how to develop a step-by-step approach.

PAPER 4   LISTENING COMPREHENSION

WHAT DOES IT TEST?

This paper tests your ability to understand spoken English when you hear it. It does not test your written English. This means that small spelling mistakes in your answers do not matter, provided that the examiner can understand what you have written. The recordings with this book will help you to get used to a variety of voices.

SUGGESTED METHOD OF WORKING

It is probably best to begin by working on one passage at a time. Get used to following the instructions on the tape. You can start writing your answers at any time. Most students write in the easy ones as they listen, then use the pause at the end of the passage to fill in the others. This means that they can use the repeat of the passage to check.

Use the Tapescript printed in the Key only *after* you have marked your answers. You will probably find it helpful to play the tape as you read. This will help you understand more exactly what you hear.

Remember that it is not always necessary to understand every word in order to answer the questions correctly.

PART TWO Practice Tests

Practice Test 1

PAPER 1 READING COMPREHENSION (1 hour)

Answer all questions. Indicate your choice of answer in every case **on the separate**
answer sheet *already given out, which should show your name and examination*
index number. Follow carefully the instructions about how to record your answers.
Give **one answer only** *to each question. Marks will not be deducted for wrong*
answers: your total score on this test will be the number of correct answers you give.

SECTION A

In this section you must choose the word or phrase which best completes each
sentence. **On your answer sheet** *indicate the letter A, B, C or D against the number*
of each item 1 to 25 for the word or phrase you choose.

1 It's a good idea to see your doctor regularly for ....
   A a revision   B a control   C an investigation   D a check-up

2 I lost too much money betting at the races last time, so you won't ....
   me to go again.
   A convince   B impress   C persuade   D urge

3 Last year the potato harvest was very disappointing, but this year it looks as
   though we shall have a better ....
   A product   B outcome   C amount   D crop

4 The shop assistant was .... helpful, but she felt he could have given her
   more advice.
   A entirely   B exactly   C quite   D totally

5 When the starter gave the .... all the competitors in the race began to
   run round the track.
   A signal   B warning   C shot   D show

6 It's an awful .... your wife couldn't come. I was looking forward to
   meeting her.
   A harm   B sorrow   C shame   D shock

7 .... from Bill, all the students said they would go.
   A Except   B Only   C Apart   D Separate

8 The new manager explained to the staff that she hoped to .... new
procedures to save time and money.
A manufacture   B establish   C control   D restore

9 There is a fault at our television station. Please do not .... your set.
A change   B adjust   C repair   D switch

10 He was an .... writer because he persuaded many people to see the
truth of his ideas.
A ordinary   B influential   C unlimited   D accurate

11 The meal was excellent; the pears were particularly ....
A flavoured   (B) delicious   C tasteful   D desirable

12 Workers who do not obey the safety regulations will be ....
immediately.
A refused   B rejected   C disapproved   D dismissed

13 He was in .... of a large number of men.
A management   B leadership   C charge   D direction

14 .... goes the bus; now we will have to walk!
A On time   B At once   C There   D Early

15 When he retired from his job the directors .... him with a clock.
A offered   B pleased   C satisfied   D presented

16 He had to leave his family .... when he went abroad to work.
A at a loss   B behind   C out   D at all costs

17 I am very .... in the information you have given me.
A concerned   B surprised   C interesting   D interested

18 When I went to talk to the manager, he told me he could only .... me a
few minutes.
A provide   (B) spare   C hear   D let

19 I saw a thief take Norman's wallet so I ran .... him, but I didn't catch
him.
A into   B after   C over   D near

20 If it's raining tomorrow, we shall have to .... the match till Sunday.
A put off   B cancel   C play   D put away

21 It is usually better not to .... things, in case they are not returned.
A lend   B offer   C borrow   D lose

20

22 He opened the letter without .... to read the address on the envelope.
    A worrying   B caring   C fearing   D bothering

23 There was a big hole in the road which .... the traffic.
    A held up   B kept down   C stood back   D sent back

24 The boy fell into the river and was .... along by the fast current.
    A caught   B swept   C thrown   D swung

25 The old sailing boat was .... without trace during the fierce storm.
    A lost   B crashed   C disappeared   D vanished

SECTION B

In this section you will find after each of the passages a number of questions or unfinished statements about the passage, each with four suggested answers or ways of finishing. You must choose the one which you think fits best. **On your answer sheet, indicate the letter A, B, C or D against the number of each item 26–40 for the answer you choose. Give one answer only to each question. Read each passage right through before choosing your answers.*

FIRST PASSAGE

Frances Wingate had not been to Tockley for many years – she could not remember how many. Her grandfather had died when she was fourteen. Her grandmother had died ten years later, but she had been out of the country at the time and had not gone to the funeral. In fact, after her grandfather's death she had hardly visited Tockley at all, she now remembered guiltily: the place had begun to depress her. She could no longer stand the slow pace, the quietness, the emptiness, the very things that had charmed her as a small child, and her grandmother had turned odd and difficult to live with, even more bad-tempered than she had been when younger, even more given to sudden bursts of anger and long silences.

    She thought of it, then as now, as 'going to Tockley', but the house wasn't really in Tockley: it was about six miles out, a distance that had then seemed enormous, as it had to be travelled by bus. The town was a medium-sized ordinary town, with much light industry; it was easy enough to get to, but it was the kind of place one goes through, rather than stops at. Frances had booked a room at the Railway Hotel, because it was next to the station, and because her guide-book said it was well run and that the food was quite good. She looked out of the window of the train and wondered what she remembered of the town. Little, she thought. It hadn't meant much to her grandparents: they went there once a fortnight to shop, depending otherwise on the shop in the nearest village and on what they produced in their own garden. There was a famous church, rising out of the flat plain, which could be seen for miles: her guide-book described it with some excitement, but she didn't remember that she had ever been in it. She remembered the wool shop, the shoe shop, the grocer's a little. It had probably all changed by now.

The cottage, too, had probably changed. She remembered it in great detail. It had been the one fixed point in her childhood; for her parents had always been moving from one house to another as her father had been promoted from one academic post to the next; five years here, three years there, had been the pattern. Granny Ollerenshaw, in the cottage, had been immovable, unchanged and unchanging. They called it Eel Cottage: over the doorway there was a square sign which announced EEL 1779. For years Frances had thought that this meant the fish which lived in muddy ditches; only later, looking more closely, did she realize that the mysterious word must have been the builder's or owner's initials. The cottage was a basic cottage, the kind that small children draw: low, a door in the middle, two windows downstairs, two windows upstairs. It was built of red brick, the brick of the district, with a red-tiled steep roof.

26 Why didn't Frances remember very much about Tockley?
    A There was nothing special in the town.
    B She had only been there once or twice.
    C She had been abroad for a long time.
    D The town had changed a great deal since her childhood.

27 Where was Frances' grandparents' house?
    A On the edge of Tockley.
    B Near the shops in Tockley.
    C In a village on a bus route from Tockley.
    D In the countryside some miles from Tockley.

28 Why was Frances' grandparents' house called 'Eel Cottage'?
    A Eels used to be common in the area.
    B Someone's initials had spelt the word 'Eel'.
    C The first owner had been called Mr Eel.
    D No one knew why.

29 Why did Frances stop visiting the cottage regularly?
    A She had been leading a very busy life.
    B She had quarrelled with her grandmother.
    C She had come to dislike the place.
    D She had lost touch with her family.

30 Why had her grandparents' house meant a lot to Frances as a child?
    A She had been brought up happily there.
    B The shape and colour of the house had attracted her.
    C She had felt things would never change there.
    D She had been lonely as a child.

SECOND PASSAGE

Trees should only be pruned when there is a good and clear reason for doing so and, fortunately, the number of such reasons is small. Pruning involves the cutting away of overgrown and unwanted branches, and the inexperienced gardener can be encouraged by the thought that more damage results from doing it unnecessarily than from leaving the tree to grow in its own way.

First, pruning may be done to make sure that trees have a desired shape or size. The object may be to get a tree of the right height, and at the same time to help the growth of small side branches which will thicken its appearance or give it a special shape. Secondly, pruning may be done to make the tree healthier. You may cut out diseased or dead wood, or branches that are rubbing against each other and thus causing wounds. The health of a tree may be encouraged by removing branches that are blocking up the centre and so preventing the free movement of air.

One result of pruning is that an open wound is left on the tree and this provides an easy entry for disease, but it is a wound that will heal. Often there is a race between the healing and the disease as to whether the tree will live or die, so that there is a period when the tree is at risk. It should be the aim of every gardener to reduce that risk of death as far as possible. It is essential to make the area which has been pruned smooth and clean, for healing will be slowed down by roughness. You should allow the cut surface to dry for a few hours and then paint it with one of the substances available from garden shops produced especially for this purpose. Pruning is usually done in winter, for then you can see the shape of the tree clearly without interference from the leaves and it is, too, very unlikely that the cuts you make will bleed. If this does happen, it is, of course, impossible to paint them properly.

31 Pruning should be done to
   A   make the tree grow taller.
   B   improve the shape of the tree.
   C   get rid of the small branches.
   D   make the small branches thicker.

32 Trees become unhealthy if the gardener
   A   allows too many branches to grow in the middle.
   B   does not protect them from the wind.
   C   forces them to grow too quickly.
   D   damages some of the small side branches.

33 Why is a special substance painted on the tree?
   A   to make a wound smooth
   B   to prevent disease entering a wound
   C   to cover a rough surface
   D   to help a wound to dry

34 A good gardener prunes a tree
    A   at intervals throughout the year.
    B   as quickly as possible.
    Ⓒ   occasionally when necessary.
    D   regularly every winter.

35 What was the author's purpose when writing this passage?
    A   to give practical instructions for pruning a tree
    Ⓑ   to give a general description of pruning
    C   to explain how trees develop diseases
    D   to discuss different methods of pruning

THIRD PASSAGE

You go to a bookstall to choose some books for a long train journey. You pick some up and read what it says about them on the back covers.
Read the following extracts from the book descriptions and then answer the questions.

Book A

...The Roman Emperor Claudius writes the inside story of his public life. Men classed him as a pitiful fool. But the actions he describes are far from foolish. Reluctantly crowned Emperor, he appears as a man whose errors came from good nature and innocence. It is the common people and the common soldiers who help him to repair the damage done by the Emperor Caligula by conquering Britain, and who stand by him in his final hard judgement on his unfaithful wife, Messalina.

This is one of the finest historical reconstructions published this century...

Book B

...A fortune-teller once told Mary (as the author calls herself in this book): "You are going to be loved by people you've never seen and never will see".
That statement came true when she published her delightful and exact record of country life at the end of the last century – a record in which she describes the fast-dissolving England of farm-worker and country tradesman and colours her picture with the cheerful courage and the rare pleasures that marked a self-sufficient world of work and poverty...

Book C

..."Leave it to my man, Johnson," Cecil used to say, whether the problem was the colour of a shirt, the shape of a hat, the style of a coat. What did it matter if Johnson tended to take charge of his life and that without his approval his employer could not even grow a moustache? Was he not always there for him to lean on in moments of difficulty? And such moments were frequent in the leisured life of Cecil and his friends in the London of the first motor buses.

Book D

> ...The novel is the story of a man for whom both real life and university research have lost their meaning. Separated from his over-emotional wife, Gerald Middleton is painfully aware that the centre of his life is empty. But the world is reaching out for him again...
>
> Gerald is the only person still alive who was present when Bishop Eorpwald's grave was opened and the strange wooden figure found which has offended, puzzled and fascinated students of early English history for years. But he also keeps another even worse secret...

36   Which book will probably be light and humorous?
   A   Book A
   B   Book B
   C   Book C
   D   Book D

37   Which book seems to be set in the present day?
   A   Book A
   B   Book B
   C   Book C
   D   Book D

38   From the information given here, the Emperor Claudius appears to have been
   A   a foolish ruler.
   B   an ambitious man.
   C   a successful general.
   D   a forgiving husband.

39   Gerald Middleton appears to be a
   A   professor of history.
   B   private detective.
   C   writer of crime stories.
   D   university student.

40   What was the relationship between Johnson and Cecil?
   A   Johnson ordered Cecil to do things.
   B   Johnson never questioned orders.
   C   Cecil depended on Johnson.
   D   Cecil paid Johnson well.

PAPER 2   COMPOSITION   (1½ hours)

Write **two only** *of the following composition exercises. Your answers must follow exactly the instructions given and must be of between 120 and 180 words each.*

1   You came to London a month ago to study English. Write a letter to your parents, telling them about the course you are taking and some of the difficulties you have encountered.

2   The students in your college think the food and service in the canteen are very poor. The Principal of the college has agreed to listen to your complaints and to discuss suggestions for improvement. Write what you would say to him.

3   You were visiting some friends in their flat late one evening when you heard someone shout 'Fire'! Describe what happened next.

4   Unemployment, especially among young people, is a serious problem in many countries today. What can be done about it? Do you think traditional ideas about work should be changed?

5   Based on your reading of any one of these books, write on *one* of the following.

JANE AUSTEN: *Sense and Sensibility*
Who is Colonel Brandon, and what part does he play in the novel?

G. B. SHAW: *Arms and the Man*
When Bluntschli leaves after hiding in Raina's bedroom, she gives him her father's old coat to disguise him. Explain what happens to the coat after that.

GRAHAM GREENE: *The Third Man*
There are two funerals in this story and both are for Harry Lime. Explain how this came about.

PAPER 3   USE OF ENGLISH   (2 hours)

1   *Fill each of the numbered blanks in the following passage. Use only* **one** *word in each space.*

Carter was usually able to catch the 6.35 train from Euston. This brought ....(1) to the town where he lived at 7.12. His bicycle waited ....(2) him at the station – the ticket-collector always looked ....(3) it for him. Then he ....(4) home, changing his route from day to day. He crossed the canal ....(5), turned ....(6) the church and up the hill to his small, semi-detached house ....(7) Queens Road. He had ....(8) it on his return to England and although he ....(9) have afforded a much bigger house, he had no wish to draw attention to himself ....(10) the source of his income. He always arrived home at 7.30, unless he had ....(11) Sarah, his wife, to say that he would be ....(12) late. There was just time ....(13) say goodnight to his baby son and have a whisky or two before dinner at 8.00.

When he ....(14) the door of his house he saw that the hall was empty, and there was no sound from the kitchen. He noticed at ....(15) that the whisky bottle was not standing ready on the small table in the living-room. The habit of years had ....(16) broken and Carter felt anxious. He called, 'Sarah!' but there was ....(17) reply. He had always, ...(18) they returned ....(19) England, known that this moment ....(20) come, and he tried not to panic.

2 *Finish each of the following sentences in such a way that it means exactly the same as the sentence printed before it.*

EXAMPLE: I haven't enjoyed myself so much for years.

ANSWER: It's years *since I enjoyed myself so much.*

a) 'Why don't you put a better lock on the door, Barry?' said John.

John suggested ~~that~~ that Barry should put a better lock

b) Although both his legs were broken in the crash, he managed to get out of the car before it exploded.

Despite his (two) legs were broken in the crash,

c) I haven't eaten this kind of food before.

This is the first time ~~to eat~~ this kind of food.
I have eaten.

d) After fighting the fire for twelve hours the firemen succeeded in putting it out.

The firemen managed to ~~succeed~~ in putting it out for twelve hours.
put it out
the fire

e) The architect has drawn plans for an extension to the house.

Plans have been drawn for an exten

f) In Stratford-on-Avon, we saw Shakespeare's birthplace.

We saw the house in which Shakespear ~~had been~~ born
was

g) It isn't necessary for you to finish by Saturday.

You don't have to finish by Sat

h) 'How many survivors are there?' asked the journalist.

The journalist wanted to know How many survivors there ~~are.~~
were

i) It was such rotten meat that it had to be thrown away.

The meat was so rotten that it had to be —

j) It is essential that Professor Van Helsing is met at the airport.
must be

Professor Van Helsing must be met

3   Complete the following sentences with **one** appropriate word connected with the subject of **money**.

EXAMPLE: His *salary* is paid into his bank account every month.

a) You can't pay by cheque or credit card. They only accept ....~~cheque~~. cash .

b) What is the ..exchange.. rate of the pound today?

c) During the sale the shop will give a 20% ..discount.. on all purchases over £100.

d) Because of losing his job, he can hardly find the money to re-pay his bank
    ....loan........
    overdraft .

e) If you invest £100,000 in our bank for one year, we will pay you 10% ..interest..

4   Complete the following sentences with an expression formed from **turn**.

EXAMPLE: They expected two hundred people to come to the meeting but only seventy turned *up*.

a) The radio is too loud. Turn it ...down......

b) The concert was so popular that people who had not bought tickets in advance were turned ...away.... at the door.

c) The large vase in which he had kept his umbrella for many years turned ..out........ to be a valuable piece of Chinese pottery.

d) She was standing at the end of the pier looking out to sea and I waited for her to turn ...~~~~........ so that I could see her face.
    (a)round.

e) Without any warning the dog, which had been lying quietly on the grass, turned ...on........ the postman and bit him.
    ?

5 *Make all the changes and additions necessary to produce, from the following sets of words and phrases, sentences which together make a complete letter. Note carefully from the example what kind of alterations need to be made. Write each sentence in the space provided.*

EXAMPLE: I / wonder / why you / not / reply / last letter.

ANSWER: I was wondering why you had not replied to my last letter.

Dear Sir,

I / very surprised / letter / I receive / you this morning.

a) _I was very surprise at letter I received you this morning._

In it / say / I not pay / book / send / one month ago.

b) _In it it says I havent pay for the book which sent one month ago._

You say / I / send / money immediately.

c) _You say I must send you money immediately._

In fact / I return / book / you / same day / receive.

d) _In fact I return the book to you same day I received it._

I not return / because / not want.

e) _I didnt return it because I didnt want it._

But because / book / be / poor condition / several torn pages.

f) _But because book was in poor condition with several torn pages._

I send / letter / that time / ask you / send / perfect copy / same book.

g) _I sent you the letter that time to ask you to send the perfect copy of the same book_

I hope / you do that and / not have / write / you again / this matter.

h) _I hope you'll do that and I'll not have to write to you again about this matter._

Yours faithfully,
Samuel Johnson

31

6   *Read the following passages about some proposed property developments in the town of Melchester, and look also at the instructions on page 33.*

From 'An Architectural Guide to Britain':

MELCHESTER (pop. 65,000)
The town is attractively situated on the River Ouse and dates from the ninth century. Despite its great age the town has few buildings of interest. In the last ten years there has been a lot of 'development' – new Town Hall, library, bus station, railway station. Perhaps the only building in the town which the visitor should make a point of seeing is the Old Grammar School. Built in the early seventeenth century by a rich local merchant, Sir William Waller, it is one of the oldest school buildings in England and is a perfect example of the style of that period. There is a magnificent exterior and inside some fine ceilings and panelled walls.

From the 'Melchester Times':

OLD SCHOOL TO MOVE TO NEW SITE

MR DAVID WALLER, Chairman of the Governors of the Old Grammar School has announced that a new school will be built on the outskirts of Melchester. To raise money for this the Old Grammar School is to be sold. 'The school is on a prime site in the centre of town. It may look beautiful from the outside but inside it is in a terrible state: It is dark and gloomy and there is little fresh air or light. It is more suitable for rabbits than schoolboys. It is costing us too much to keep on repairing it'. He added that Mega Properties had made a 'substantial offer' for the site.

MEMO: URGENT

FROM: Lord Grabbit, Chairman of Mega Properties

TO: Peter Smooth, Publicity Officer, Mega Properties

   Apparently certain people in Melchester are opposed to our plans to demolish the Old Grammar School and build a new shopping centre on the site and are calling for the Minister of the Environment to hold an inquiry. Please prepare some publicity material to be sent to local newspapers and influential local people in the town. Point out that both the construction of the centre and the shops themselves will provide jobs for the people of Melchester where there is a lot of unemployment. Explain that the interior of the school is in such a poor state that it cannot be used for any purpose. The site is too important to have an empty or underused building on it and more people will come to shop in the shopping centre than come to look at the school.

To the editor of the 'Melchester Times':

Dear Sir,
   We are very disturbed by reports that the Old Grammar School is to be demolished by Mega Properties. Our town has already lost many of its historic old buildings which have been replaced by boring examples of modern architecture (several of them built by Mega Properties). The Old Grammar School is a building of great historical and architectural significance – to destroy it would be an act of vandalism. We are in favour of keeping the building and renovating the interior which could be used for offices, evening classes, exhibitions, a meeting place for local clubs and societies and many other purposes.
Yours faithfully,

JOHN KEEP,
Chairman,
Melchester
Heritage Society

To the editor of the
'Melchester Times':

Dear Sir,
I have been following with great interest the debate in your columns between those who wish to keep the Old Grammar School and those who wish to see a new shopping centre on the site. May I suggest a compromise? Most people seem to agree that it is the exterior of the building which is beautiful. Why not keep the exterior frontage and build a shopping centre behind it, demolishing only the interior of the school? That way we could have the shopping centre and the best part of the school. As an architect, I know that this can be done.
Yours faithfully,
JOHN NASH

MEMO:

FROM: Lord Grabbit

TO: Peter Smooth

Support seems to be growing for the idea of keeping the exterior of the Old Grammar School. Attack this idea vigorously! It will be far cheaper and more convenient for us to demolish the entire school and start building on an empty site.

There are three proposals concerning the future of the Old Grammar School at Melchester. Describe each one in one sentence.

1   To demolish the old Gram. school to provide jobs The site is ~~too~~ important.

2   keeping the building and renovating the interior. which could be used for offices, evening classes exhibitions, a meeting place

3   building shop behind ~~building~~ school and and keeping the exterior frontage and demolishing only the interior.

Which do you think is the best proposal? Complete the following paragraph in not more than 100 words, giving reasons for the one you have chosen and taking into account its advantages and disadvantages.

I think the best proposal is to ....

....

....

....

....

PAPER 4   LISTENING COMPREHENSION
(about 30 minutes)

FIRST PART

In the table below there are three people and eight statements about them. Decide which statements apply to each person and tick (√) the appropriate boxes.

		the woman	the man	the woman's friend at university
1	likes loud music at night			
2	likes working early in the morning			
3	likes listening to classical music			
4	likes to set a time limit			
5	likes to finish a specific topic in a day			
6	needs a lot of coffee when working			
7	sleeps during the afternoon			
8	likes to listen to loud music on the radio			

SECOND PART

For questions 9–20 tick (√) whether the statements are true or false.

	True	False
9 'Tell All' is a 'phone-in' programme.		
10 There were lots of letters about 'Weather Tomorrow'.		
11 Mr J. Jones disagreed with Professor Strong's theory.		
12 Mrs Marsh would like daily weather forecasts improved.		
13 Changeable weather is preferred by a Scottish listener.		
14 Food is a popular topic amongst listeners.		
15 On Mondays there's a cookery series for men.		
16 The Producer of 'Men in the Kitchen' is a woman.		
17 Listeners will eventually be doing more difficult cookery.		
18 The student has supplied her address.		
19 Libraries will definitely charge 20 pence per book.		
20 Spectacles and false teeth are free.		

THIRD PART

Fill in the gaps 21–25 on the programme board shown below.

	PROGRAMMES BEGINNING		
	Weekdays	**Sundays**	**Prices**
ABC 1 'The Captain's Lady'	1.00	㉑	
(15 Cert.)	4.05	6.40	£2.10
	7.10		
ABC 2 'Starfighters'	1.10	3.30	£2.10
(U Cert.)	4.20	6.30	children under 16
	7.40	㉒ £.....................	
ABC 3 ㉓		,㉔	4.20
(15 Cert.)	4.45	7.10	£2.10
	7.30		

REDUCED RATES FOR OVER-SIXTIES FOR AFTERNOON PERFORMANCES.
LATE SHOW ON ㉕ .... : 'THE CAPTAIN'S LADY'
  DOORS OPEN 10.45 P.M.

FOURTH PART

For questions 26–30 tick (√) whether you think the statements are true or false.

	True	False
26 You can hear the final instalment again next Friday morning.		
27 The next programme on Radio 4 is called 'Helston in Cornwall'.		
28 You can hear the football commentary at 9 o'clock.		
29 The programme 'Would you credit it?' is on Radio 3 at 10 o'clock.		
30 If you want to listen to the 'London Pop Spectacular', turn over to Radio 1.		

Practice Test 2

PAPER 1   READING COMPREHENSION   (1 hour)

Answer all questions. Indicate your choice of answer in every case **on the separate answer sheet** *already given out, which should show your name and examination index number. Follow carefully the instructions about how to record your answers. Give* **one answer only** *to each question. Marks will not be deducted for wrong answers: your total score on this test will be the number of correct answers you give.*

SECTION A

In this section you must choose the word or phrase which best completes each sentence. **On your answer sheet** *indicate the letter, A, B, C or D, against the number of each item 1 to 25 for the word or phrase you choose.*

1   You can learn as much theory as you like, but you only master a skill by
    .... it a lot.
    A practising   B training   C exercising   D doing

2   Some people think it is .... to use long and little-known words.
    A clever   B intentional   C skilled   D sensitive

3   The Chairman was so angry with the committee that he decided to ....
    from it.
    A cancel   B postpone   C resign   D prevent

4   The explorers walked all the way along the river from its mouth to its
    ....
    A cause   B well   C source   D outlet

5   He was afraid of losing his suitcase so he tied a .... on it on which he
    had written his name and address.
    A badge   B mark   C label   D notice

6   He enjoyed the dessert so much that he accepted a second .... when it
    was offered.
    A load   B pile   C helping   D sharing

⟫→

7   He soon received promotion, for his superiors realized that he was a man of considerable ....
    A ability   B possibility   C future   D opportunity

8   Is there a bank where I can .... these pounds for dollars?
    A exchange   B turn   C alter   D arrange

9   To our .... , Geoffrey's illness proved not to be as serious as we had feared.
    A anxiety   B eyes   C relief   D judgement

10 The author had qualified as a doctor but later gave up the .... of medicine for full-time writing.
    A practice   B treatment   C procedure   D prescription

11 Don't touch the cat, he may .... you.
    A kick   B tear   C scream   D scratch

12 Buy the new .... of soap now on sale: it is softer than all others!
    A model   B brand   C mark   D manufacture

13 The chief of police said that he saw no .... between the six murders.
    A joint   B connection   C communication   D join

14 The safety committee's report recommended that all medicines should be kept out of the .... of children.
    A hold   B hand   C reach   D grasp

15 In the jar there was a .... which looked like jam.
    A substance   B material   C solid   D powder

16 He was surprised that her English was so .... as she had never been to England.
    A definite   B liquid   C fluent   D national

17 He is very stubborn, so it will be difficult to .... him to go.
    A persuade   B suggest   C make   D prevent

18 He put a .... against the tree and climbed up to pick the apples.
    A scale   B staircase   C grade   D ladder

19 It's six years now since the Socialists came to .... in that country.
    A power   B force   C control   D command

20 You're looking very pale — do you .... sick?
    A fall   B faint   C feel   D become

21 He stood on one leg, ... against the wall, while he took off his shoe.
   A stopping   B staying   C leaning   D supporting

22 In a greengrocer's shop there is a lot of .... when fruit and vegetables
   are not sold.
   A rot   B waste   C ruin   D rest

23 After the party the children were allowed to finish off the ....
   sandwiches and cakes.
   A additional   B leaving   C remaining   D left

24 When the time came to .... the bill at the hotel she found her purse had
   been stolen.
   A pay   B pay out   C pay for   D pay up

25 When the manager went to Canada on business his .... took over all
   his duties.
   A caretaker   B officer   C deputy   D commander

SECTION B

*In this section you will find after each of the passages a number of questions or
unfinished statements about the passage, each with four suggested answers or ways of
finishing. You must choose the one which you think fits best.* **On your answer sheet,**
*indicate the letter A, B, C or D against the number of each item 26–40 for the answer
you choose. Give one answer only to each question. Read each passage right through
before choosing your answers.*

FIRST PASSAGE

It was on one of the hottest August days – the fourth, and at twelve o'clock exactly,
for a church clock was striking the hour – that a short, heavily-built woman of about
fifty, carrying a shopping bag, came out from the darkness of an old storehouse
where she worked every morning as a checker, and set off along the narrow grey
street to a bus stop. Most of the factories and offices in the town were closed for two
weeks but the storehouse, which held foodstuffs and other goods that did not keep,
had remained open during the holidays. The heat, made worse by the heavy smell
of petrol from the main street near by and undisturbed by the slightest current of
cooler air, enveloped her. She was neither dressed nor built for energetic activity on
a hot day, being very short indeed, and fat, so that she had to roll a little in order to
get along. Her tight black dress was worn without a belt or any ornaments other
than a large metal cross, well fingered but of no special value, which hung on a

white ribbon around her neck. Her cracked shoes made loud footsteps in the silence of the empty street of closed buildings. The worn old bag she carried caused her to lean over slightly to her right as she walked, but it was clear that she was used to carrying such heavy weights.

Reaching her usual bus stop, she put down her bag and rested. Then, suddenly conscious of being watched, she turned quickly round and looked sharply upward at the tall man behind her.

He was the only other person waiting, and indeed, at that moment, the only other person in the street. She had never spoken to him, yet his face was already familiar to her: so big, so uncertain, so sweaty. She had seen it yesterday, and the day before, and for all she knew, the day before that as well. For the last three or four days anyway, this great nervous lump of a man, waiting for a bus or hanging about on the footpath outside the storehouse, had become a figure of the street for her; and what was more, a figure of a certain definite type, though she had yet to put her finger on exactly which type it was. More than once, she had felt his interest in her and she had wondered whether he was a policeman.

26   Why were there so few people about in this particular street at midday?
     A   It was too hot to be outside.
     B   Most workers were on holiday.
     C   The lunch-time break had not yet started.
     D   Not many people lived in the area now.

27   What was the woman wearing?
     A   a dark dress with a lot of jewellery
     B   a loose summer dress
     C   a dress with a white collar
     D   a plain and simple dress

28   The woman was hindered in walking by
     A   her tight dress.
     B   her heavy necklace.
     C   her round shape.
     D   her worn-out shoes.

29   The woman turned round because
     A   she heard someone coming.
     B   she thought the bus was due.
     C   she remembered about her bag.
     D   she felt someone looking at her.

30   Why did the woman recognize the man by the bus stop?
     A   He was the local policeman.
     B   He travelled on the bus regularly.
     C   He had been near the storehouse before.
     D   He was like someone she knew well.

SECOND PASSAGE

The pig was the last animal to be fully domesticated by the farmer. Unlike the cow and the sheep, it is not a grass-eater. Its ancient home was the forest, where it searched for different kinds of food, such as nuts, roots and dead animals, and found in the bushes protection for its almost hairless body from extremes of sun and cold. For many centuries the farmer allowed it to continue there, leaving his pigs to look after themselves most of the time. As the woodlands began to shrink, the pig slowly began to be kept on the farm itself. But it did not finally come into a shed, where it was fed on waste food from the farm and the house, until the eighteenth century.

The pig, then, became a farm animal in the age of agricultural improvement in Britain in the eighteenth century, but it was given little attention by special animal breeders, for the major farmers of the time preferred to develop the larger kinds of animal. There were, however, various less well-known farmers interested in pigs and they based their improvements on new types of pig from overseas. These were the Chinese pig, and its various relatives, including the Neapolitan pig, which were descended from Chinese pigs that had found their way to the Mediterranean in ancient times. These were very different from the thin and leggy British woodland pigs. They were wider and squarer, with shorter legs and flatter faces, and they matured earlier and produced more delicate meat. By the end of the eighteenth century these overseas pigs had influenced the colour, shape and characteristics of the native British pig a great deal.

In the early nineteenth century, all sorts and conditions of pig-farmer worked at improving all sorts and conditions of pig. Many of the special pigs they developed are now forgotten, but by the end of the century they had established most of the kinds we know in Britain today.

31 In their original wild state pigs
    A   ate the same food as other animals.
    B   wandered across the plains.
    C   lived among trees.
    D   did not go near cows or sheep.

32 Why were pigs not fully domesticated in Britain until the eighteenth century?
    A   They could find food for themselves well enough in woodlands.
    B   There was no suitable food for them on most farms.
    C   It was difficult to develop improved types of pig.
    D   They did not grow well when kept indoors.

33 The passage tells us that in the age of agricultural improvement in Britain in the eighteenth century
    A   very fat pigs were developed.
    B   British types of pig were replaced with overseas ones.
    C   pigs received less attention than other animals.
    D   important breeders concentrated on pigs.   ⟫→

34 How did Chinese and Neapolitan pigs differ from native British pigs?
    A They were taller.
    B They had shorter noses.
    C They had stronger legs.
    D They were rounder.

THIRD PASSAGE

Three friends, Jean, Helen and Emma, have gone on a week's holiday together.
They send these three postcards to Ann, who works in the same office.

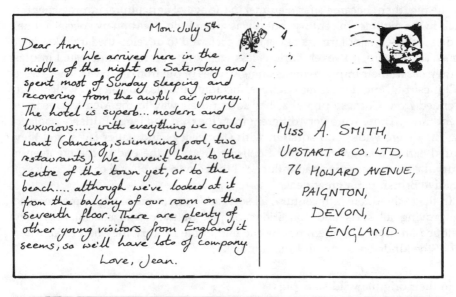

Mon. July 5th

Dear Ann,
      We arrived here in the
middle of the night on Saturday and
spent most of Sunday sleeping and
recovering from the awful air journey.
The hotel is superb... modern and
luxurious.... with everything we could
want (dancing, swimming pool, two
restaurants). We haven't been to the
centre of the town yet, or to the
beach.... although we've looked at it
from the balcony of our room on the
seventh floor. There are plenty of
other young visitors from England it
seems, so we'll have lots of company.
               Love, Jean.

Miss A. SMITH,
UPSTART & CO. LTD,
76 HOWARD AVENUE,
PAIGNTON,
DEVON,
ENGLAND.

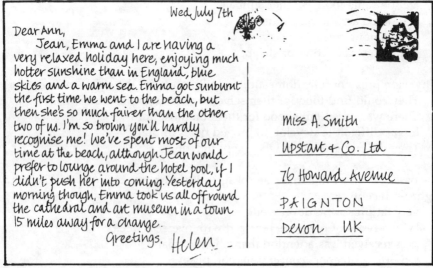

Wed, July 7th

Dear Ann,
      Jean, Emma and I are having a
very relaxed holiday here, enjoying much
hotter sunshine than in England, blue
skies and a warm sea. Emma got sunburnt
the first time we went to the beach, but
then she's so much fairer than the other
two of us. I'm so brown you'll hardly
recognise me! We've spent most of our
time at the beach, although Jean would
prefer to lounge around the hotel pool, if I
didn't push her into coming. Yesterday
morning though, Emma took us all off round
the cathedral and art museum in a town
15 miles away for a change.
               Greetings. Helen

Miss A. Smith
Upstart & Co. Ltd
76 Howard Avenue
PAIGNTON
Devon   UK

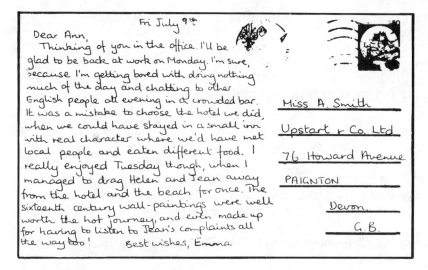

Fri July 9th

Dear Ann,
    Thinking of you in the office. I'll be glad to be back at work on Monday. I'm sure, because I'm getting bored with doing nothing much of the day and chatting to other English people all evening in a crowded bar. It was a mistake to choose the hotel we did, when we could have stayed in a small inn with real character where we'd have met local people and eaten different food. I really enjoyed Tuesday though, when I managed to drag Helen and Jean away from the hotel and the beach for once. The sixteenth century wall-paintings were well worth the hot journey, and even made up for having to listen to Jean's complaints all the way too!   Best wishes, Emma

Miss A. Smith

Upstart + Co. Ltd

76 Howard Avenue

PAIGNTON

Devon.

G.B.

35   Where are the three friends staying?
     A   a modern hotel in the south of England
     B   a large hotel in a seaside town
     C   a small hotel right by the beach
     D   a luxury hotel in an historic town

36   What is the weather like?
     A   too warm for two of them
     B   cool in the evening
     C   too warm for all of them
     D   sunny and hot

37   Which of the three friends seems to get her own way about what they are going to do most of the time?
     A   Jean   B   Helen   C   Emma
     D   no one more than the others

38   What does Helen most enjoy?
     A   relaxing by the pool
     B   sunbathing on the beach
     C   talking to English people
     D   visiting historic places

39   Who likes the hotel where they are staying the best?
     A   Jean   B   Helen   C   Emma
     D   Two of them like it equally

40   Why will Emma be glad to get back to the office?
     A   the beach is too crowded
     B   the hotel is too expensive
     C   she is finding the holiday dull
     D   she is beginning to dislike Jean and Helen

PAPER 2   COMPOSITION   (1½ hours)

*Write **two only** of the following composition exercises. Your answers must follow exactly the instructions given and must be of between 120 and 180 words each.*

1   You need a job for three months in the summer, and you have seen an advertisement in a newspaper about a temporary job as a tourist guide in your town or city. Write a letter applying for the post.

2   You are looking after some young children. Tell them a story you enjoyed when you were a child.

3   'I woke up and started to cough. The room was full of smoke.' Continue the story, describing your escape from the building.

4   'Most people spend too much time watching television nowadays.' Do you agree?

5   Based on your reading of any one of these books, write on *one* of the following.

JANE AUSTEN: *Sense and Sensibility*
What have you found especially interesting about Jane Austen's attitude to marriage?

G. B. SHAW: *Arms and the Man*
Why does Captain Bluntschli return to the Petkoffs' house after the peace treaty? Explain how this second visit affects the lives of some of the characters in the play.

GRAHAM GREENE: *The Third Man*
'There was something wrong about Lime's death, something the police had been too stupid to discover.' Describe Rollo Martins' attempts to investigate this 'death', until he is proved right by seeing Lime's 'ghost'.

PAPER 3   USE OF ENGLISH   (2 hours)

1   *Fill each of the numbered blanks in the following passage. Use only* **one** *word in each space.*

After we had been marching for two weeks, getting soaked by daily rains and living entirely on the ....(1) we carried with us, we found footprints. Two people were ....(2) of us and travelling fast. We followed ....(3). Each morning, when we ....(4) off again after a night's ....(5), we found their tracks in the forest nearby and ....(6) they had been watching us the ....(7) evening. One night we ....(8) gifts in the forest but they ....(9) not touched. We called out greetings ....(10) the language of the river people but we did not know ....(11) this unknown tribe were able to understand it. In any case ....(12) was no reply. We continued day ....(13) day until eventually we lost all sign of their movements. After three weeks we had almost ....(14) up hope ....(15) making contact. Then early one morning we ....(16) up to find seven men standing within a ....(17) yards of our tent. They were very small and wore nothing ....(18) a wide belt of green leaves ....(19) around their waist. Two of the men had earrings and necklaces made of bones and one carried a woven ....(20) full of roots and fruit.

2   *Finish each of the following sentences in such a way that it means exactly the same as the sentence printed before it.*

EXAMPLE: I haven't enjoyed myself so much for years.

ANSWER: It's years *since I enjoyed myself so much.*

a)   You can't visit the United States unless you get a visa.

If you ....

b)   'Can I borrow your typewriter, Janet?' asked Peter.

Peter asked if ....

c)   She started working as a secretary five years ago.

She has ....

d)   She knows a lot more about it than I do.

I don't know ....

e)   My French friend finds driving on the left difficult.

My French friend isn't ....

f)   They think the owner of the house is abroad.

The owner ....

g)   We didn't go on holiday because we didn't have enough money.

If we ....

h)   The children couldn't go swimming because the sea was very rough.

The sea was too ....

i)   What a pity you failed your driving test!

I wish ....

j)   The mechanic serviced my car last week.

I ....

3   *Complete each of the following sentences with an appropriate word or phrase made from* **time**.

   EXAMPLE: I don't like people who arrive late. I'm always *on time*.

   a)   We found out when the bus left from the ....

   b)   Did you get to the station .... to catch the train?

   c)   It was 2 a.m. .... they had finished tidying up after the party.

   d)   She wanted to complete the exercise during the lesson but she ran

   ....

   e)   My boyfriend lives in York so I can only visit him from ....

4   *Below are five groups of three words. In the spaces write* **one** *word which describes each group.*

   EXAMPLE: Coat, dress, trousers   *clothes*

   a)   Hammer, screwdriver, saw   ....

   b)   Summer, winter, spring   ....

   c)   Lunch, dinner, breakfast   ....

   d)   Table, chair, bed   ....

   e)   Car, bus, lorry   ....

5   *Make all the changes and additions necessary to produce, from the following sets of words and phrases, sentences which together make a complete letter. Note carefully from the example what kind of alterations need to be made. Write each sentence in the space provided.*

   EXAMPLE: I / wonder / why you / not / reply / last letter.

   ANSWER: I was wondering why you had not replied to my last letter.

   ⟫→

Ward 7
Great Northern Hospital
Manchester

Dear Bill,

I / expéct / you be surprise / get / letter / me.

a) I expect (that) you 'll be suprised to get the le lette from me

As / can see / address above / I be / hospital.

b) As you can see this address above , I'm in hospital.

Last Wednesday / I have / accident / when I drive / work.

c) Last W I had an accident when I drove to work

Child / run out / front / my car / and I / have / stop / sudden / that / car behind / crash / me.

d) Child ran out in front of my car and I had to stop
so suddenly that the car behind carashed into me

Luckily / I wear / seatbelt / so I / not injure badly / although / have / stay / here / next Friday.

e) Luckily I wore seatbelt so I wasn't injured badly
Although I have to stay here.

It be / very boring / I be pleased / see / if you / have / spare time.

f) It is very boring and I would be pleased
to see you if you have any spare time

Visiting hours / be / 7.00 to 9.00 / evening.

g) Visiting hours is 7:00 to 9:00 in the evening

I hope / able / come.

h) I hope you'll be able to come
you are able to

Give my regards to your family.

Yours,
John

6   *Susan Bates and Janet Peel are going to move to London to study at a college there.*
    Susan has come to London before the term starts to look for a flat for them both.
    She has visited four flats and is writing a letter to Janet to tell her about them.
    Look at the notes Susan made about each flat and then complete her letter.

112 Newton Street

Very close to college.
shops just down road.
Busy street – lots of
heavy lorries.
Big lounge (gas fire, T.V.,
phone). 1 bedroom – 2
single beds. Quite
modern, decoration o.k.
Nice bathroom.
£45 per week.

37 Manor Hill
Next to pub!
Very old flat – wallpaper
peeling off, damp patches
on ceiling. 1 bedroom.
Lounge – tiny. T.V., no phone.
Share bathroom with other
flat.
£38 per week.

9 Thornton Avenue

6 miles from college.
Modern flat on new
estate.   1 bedroom.
Gas fire in lounge – no
phone or T.V.
Bathroom – shower, no bath.
£45 per week.

25 Beech Avenue

Lovely area but 4
miles from college. Bus
stop 15 mins. walk.
Ground floor flat – use of
garden. Landlord lives
above! Central heating.
Bathroom.   2 bedrooms.
Large lounge – T.V., and
phone.
Clean, well kept.
£50 per week.

Dear Janet,

Just a quick letter to tell you what I've been doing. I went to see

four flats today and I liked one of them very much. It was in a road

called .... and I think it would suit us very well because

....

....

....

....

⟫⟫→

However it did have a couple of drawbacks. ....

....

....

....

There was another flat in .... which was nearly as good.

....

....

....

I don't think it would be as suitable for us as the other one because

....

....

....

One of the flats I saw was really dreadful. I'm amazed the landlord wanted so much for it. I doubt if you'd even consider living there because ....

....

....

I'd better finish so that I can post this. Ring me as soon as you can and let me know what you think so I can make all the arrangements.

Yours,

Susan

PAPER 4   LISTENING COMPREHENSION
(about 30 minutes)

FIRST PART

For questions 1–7 fill in the gaps in the following information sheet.

Permitted clothing ①.. and bathing costume

Best time of year: July, August, September

Best time of day: An hour and half after ②..

Style of swimming: any style acceptable

Total training: should take at least ③.. months. You should
build up your training, using the following as a rough guide: two-hour swims,
morning and evening, followed by six-hour swims, and then ten-hour swims;
and finally, in your last three weeks a minimum of ④..
hours swimming per week should be your aim.

Basic Rules

Only lanolin ⑤.. may be used as a protection against cold

Taking food and drink is ⑥.., but on no account must you

touch or hang on to the boat, as this means ⑦..

SECOND PART

For questions 8–12 tick (√) one of the boxes A, B, C or D.

8   Mr Harding serves the customer because

    A   the customer wants to speak to him.

    B   the first assistant works in another department.

    C   the first assistant is too busy.

    D   the customer knows him.

A
B
C
D

9   The customer wants to change the cassette because it

    A   has a crack in it.

    B   has caused a fault in his cassette player.

    C   has a part missing.

    D   will not work in his cassette player.

A
B
C
D

10   Mr Harding suggests that the customer is to blame because

    A   he is using the cassette in someone else's machine.

    B   the customer's machine is old.

    C   the cassette needs repairing.

    D   nobody else has made a similar complaint.

A
B
C
D

11   Mr Harding says he won't change the cassette because

    A   the shop's rule is not to change cassettes.

    B   the customer has damaged the cassette.

    C   he believes the cassette came from another shop.

    D   he believes there is nothing really wrong with it.

A
B
C
D

12   Why doesn't the manager speak to the customer?

    A   He's at lunch.

    B   He's got the whole day off.

    C   He's serving someone else.

    D   He's at a meeting.

A
B
C
D

THIRD PART

A learner driver comes across various difficulties. In the boxes numbered 13–16 enter the letter for each difficulty in the order in which they happen. The first one has been done for you.

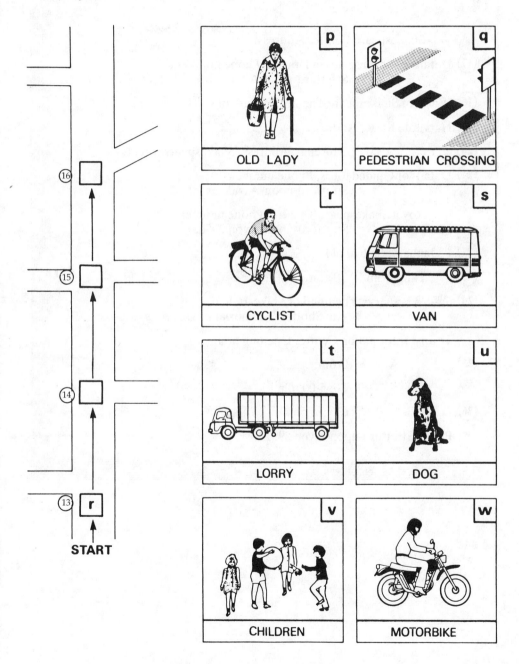

p — OLD LADY

q — PEDESTRIAN CROSSING

r — CYCLIST

s — VAN

t — LORRY

u — DOG

v — CHILDREN

w — MOTORBIKE

START

13 r
14
15
16

FOURTH PART

For questions 17–26 fill in the details about what there is to see and do in Stratford-upon-Avon, where Shakespeare was born.

Shakespeare Centre. Address: .... *Henley Street* ....

(17) Details of Shakespearian Houses. Phone number:
Stratford-upon-Avon ....

(18) World of Shakespeare Theatre. Length of show: ....

(19) Harvard House. Address: ....

(20) .... Museum. Address: Shakespeare Street.

(21) Details of Guided tours: Phone number:
Stratford-upon-Avon ....

Royal Shakespeare Theatre. Phone number:
Stratford-upon-Avon 295623

(22) 1ˢᵗ January: Sale of old ....

(23) Time from 10·30 a.m. to ....

(24) 6ᵗʰ–8ᵗʰ January: 'The Land of Make-Believe',
at Shottery Memorial ....

Tourist Information Centre. Opening hours

(25) From: ....

To: 5·00 p.m.

(26) Closed on ....

Phone Stratford-upon-Avon 293127

Practice Test 3

PAPER 1   READING COMPREHENSION   (1 hour)

Answer all questions. Indicate your choice of answer in every case **on the separate answer sheet** *already given out, which should show your name and examination index number. Follow carefully the instructions about how to record your answers. Give* **one answer only** *to each question. Marks will not be deducted for wrong answers: your total score on this test will be the number of correct answers you give.*

SECTION A

In this section you must choose the word or phrase which best completes each sentence. **On your answer sheet** *indicate the letter A, B, C or D against the number of each item 1 to 25 for the word or phrase you choose.*

1   The blue curtains began to .... after they had been hanging in the sun
    for two months.
    A fade   B die   C dissolve   D melt

2   Learners of English as a foreign language often fail to .... between
    unfamiliar sounds in that language.
    A separate   B differ   C distinguish   D solve

3   The wind blew so hard and so strongly that the windows .... in their
    frames.
    A rattled   B slapped   C flapped   D shocked

4   I have lived near the railway for so long now that I've grown .... to the
    noise of the trains.
    A accustomed   B familiar   C unconscious   D aware

5   In spite of her protests, her father .... her train for the race three hours a
    day.
    A let   B made   C insisted   D caused

6   It was impossible for her to tell the truth so she had to .... a story.
    A invent   B combine   C manage   D lie

7   The car had a .... tyre, so we had to change the wheel.
    A broken   B cracked   C bent   D flat

8 She applied for training as a pilot, but they turned her .... because of her poor eyesight.
A back   B up   C over   D down

9 The only feature .... to these two flowers is their preference for sandy soil.
A similar   B same   C shared   D common

10 The play was very long, but there were two ....
A intervals   B rests   C interruptions   D gaps

11 These old houses are going to be .... soon.
A laid out   B run down   C pulled down   D knocked out

12 She rang to make an early .... at the hairdresser's.
A order   B date   C assignment   D appointment

13 The law states that heavy goods delivery vehicles may not carry .... of more than fifteen tons.
A masses   B sizes   C measures   D loads

14 The young soldier .... a dangerous mission across the desert, although he knew that he might be killed.
A undertook   B agreed   C promised   D entered

15 You must .... that your safety belt is fastened.
A examine   B secure   C check   D guarantee

16 He .... a rare disease when he was working in the hospital.
A took   B suffered   C infected   D caught

17 My sister had a baby daughter yesterday, and she is my first ....
A nephew   B cousin   C niece   D relation

18 When he heard the joke, he burst into loud ....
A smiles   B laughter   C amusement   D enjoyment

19 The traffic lights .... to green, and the cars drove on.
A exchanged   B turned   C removed   D shone

20 It is a good idea to be .... dressed when you go for an interview.
A finely   B boldly   C smartly   D clearly

21 If we go to the market we might find a ....
A trade   B shopping   C chance   D bargain

>>>→

22 If he drinks any more beer, I don't think he'll be .... to play this
    afternoon.
    A skilled   B capable   C possible   D fit

23 That's a nice coat, and the colour .... you well.
    A fits   B matches   C shows   D suits

24 Many accidents in the home could be .... if householders gave more
    thought to safety in their houses.
    A avoided   B excluded   C protected   D preserved

25 Smoking is a very bad habit, which many people find difficult to ....
    A break   B beat   C breathe   D cough

SECTION B

*In this section you will find after each of the passages a number of questions or
unfinished statements about the passage, each with four suggested answers or ways of
finishing. You must choose the one which you think fits best.* **On your answer sheet,**
*indicate the letter A, B, C or D against the number of each item 26–40 for the answer
you choose. Give one answer only to each question. Read each passage right through
before choosing your answers.*

FIRST PASSAGE

Through a series of experiments an American scientist has obtained an
understanding of the social structure of the most complex of ant societies. The ants
examined are the only creatures other than man to have given up hunting and
collecting for a completely agricultural way of life. In their underground nests they
cultivate gardens on soil made from finely chopped leaves. This is a complex
operation requiring considerable division of labour. The workers of this type of ant
can be divided into four groups according to size. Each of the groups performs a
particular set of jobs.

The making and care of the gardens and the nursing of the young ants are done
by the smallest workers. Slightly larger workers are responsible for chopping up
leaves to make them suitable for use in the gardens and for cleaning the nest. A
third group of still larger ants do the construction work and collect fresh leaves from
outside the nest. The largest are the soldier ants, responsible for defending the nest.

To find out how good the various size-groups are at different tasks, the
scientist measured the amount of work done by the ants against the amount of
energy they used. He examined first the gathering and carrying of leaves. He
selected one of the size-groups, and then measured how efficiently these ants could
find leaves and run back to the nest. Then he repeated the experiment for each of the

other size-groups. In this way he could see whether any group could do the job more efficiently than the group normally undertaking it.

The intermediate-sized ants that normally perform this task proved to be the most efficient for their energy costs, but when the scientist examined the whole set of jobs performed by each group of ants it appeared that some sizes of worker ant were not ideally suited to the particular jobs they performed.

26 In which way are the ants different from other non-human societies?
    A   They do not need to search for food.
    B   They do not need to look for shelter.
    C   Individuals vary in social status.
    D   Individuals perform different functions.

27 It seems that smaller ants perform more of the
    A   construction tasks.
    B   domestic tasks.
    C   defensive work.
    D   heavy work.

28 'Good' (first line of third paragraph) refers to the ants'
    A   co-operation in working.
    B   sense of responsibility.
    C   efficiency in working.
    D   willingness to work hard.

29 The scientist's work was based on
    A   occasional observations.
    B   systematic observations.
    C   observations of several nests.
    D   observations of an undisturbed nest.

30 The organization of the ants has the effect of
    A   getting the most work done.
    B   dividing the work up systematically.
    C   each ant helping with all the tasks.
    D   each ant doing what it can do best.

SECOND PASSAGE

Let children learn to judge their own work. A child learning to talk does not learn by being corrected all the time: if corrected too much, he will stop talking. He notices a thousand times a day the difference between the language he uses and the language those around him use. Bit by bit, he makes the necessary changes to make his language like other people's. In the same way, children learning to do all the other things they learn to do without being taught – to walk, run, climb, whistle, ride a bicycle – compare their own performances with those of more skilled people, and slowly make the needed changes. But in school we never give a child a chance to find out his mistakes for himself, let alone correct them. We do it all for him. We act as if we thought that he would never notice a mistake unless it was pointed out to him, or correct it unless he was made to. Soon he becomes dependent on the teacher. Let him do it himself. Let him work out, with the help of other children if he wants it, what this word says, what the answer is to that problem, whether this is a good way of saying or doing this or not.

If it is a matter of right answers, as it may be in mathematics or science, give him the answer book. Let him correct his own papers. Why should we teachers waste time on such routine work? Our job should be to help the child when he tells us that he can't find the way to get the right answer. Let's end all this nonsense of grades, exams, marks. Let us throw them all out, and let the children learn what all educated persons must some day learn, how to measure their own understanding, how to know what they know or do not know.

Let them get on with this job in the way that seems most sensible to them, with our help as school teachers if they ask for it. The idea that there is a body of knowledge to be learnt at school and used for the rest of one's life is nonsense in a world as complicated and rapidly changing as ours. Anxious parents and teachers say, 'But suppose they fail to learn something essential, something they will need to get on in the world?' Don't worry! If it is essential, they will go out into the world and learn it.

31 What does the author think is the best way for children to learn things?
   A   by copying what other people do
   B   by making mistakes and having them corrected
   C   by listening to explanations from skilled people
   D   by asking a great many questions

32 What does the author think teachers do which they should not do?
   A   They give children correct answers.
   B   They point out children's mistakes to them.
   C   They allow children to mark their own work.
   D   They encourage children to copy from one another.

33 The passage suggests that learning to speak and learning to ride a bicycle are
    A   not really important skills.
    B   more important than other skills.
    C   basically different from learning adult skills.
    D   basically the same as learning other skills.

34 Exams, grades and marks should be abolished because children's progress
    should only be estimated by
    A   educated persons.
    B   the children themselves.
    C   teachers.
    D   parents.

35 The author fears that children will grow up into adults who are
    A   too independent of others.
    B   too critical of themselves.
    C   unable to think for themselves.
    D   unable to use basic skills.

THIRD PASSAGE

 # CAR HIRE

Hiring a self-drive car really adds to the enjoyment of your holiday. There are so many interesting places to visit, and if you enjoy seeing more than just the city centre there's no better way to explore than by car.

HIRE CHARGES

What's included

(a)   Unlimited mileage.

(b)   Expenses on oil, maintenance and repairs, which will be repaid on production of receipts.

(c)   Full insurance cover but exclusive of personal accident (see below) and contents.

What's not included

(a)   Personal accident insurance.

(b)   Garaging, petrol, parking and traffic fines.

CONDITIONS OF HIRE

1.   The minimum rental period at these special low prices is three days. For prices for periods of one or two days only see our representative at the hotel.

2.   Car hire **must** be booked six weeks or more before arrival in London to guarantee a car. But if you have been unable to make a booking in advance please see our representative at the hotel who may still be able to help you.

3.   The car types specified on the sheet are examples of the type of vehicles available in each price range, but a particular car cannot be guaranteed.

Upon delivery the driver(s) will be asked to sign the car hire company's Conditions of Hire.

If you decide to hire a car, just fill in the Booking Form and return it to us. A booking fee of £12 as part of the car hire cost is required.

Should you be forced to cancel your car hire booking after payment in full (two weeks before date of hire), a cancellation charge of £12 will be made.

36   What costs is a car hirer responsible for?
   A   insurance against damage to the car
   B   insurance against injury to the driver
   C   the cost of maintenance of the car
   D   the cost of repairs to the car

37   The rates for car hire are especially cheap when
    A   two days are booked.
    B   three days are booked.
    C   the booking is made in London.
    D   the booking is made from outside Britain.

38   The cost of oil
    A   has to be paid by the driver.
    B   should be charged to the company.
    C   is covered by the insurance payment.
    D   can be reclaimed by the driver.

39   What does the hire charge for a three day period depend on?
    A   the classification of the car
    B   the distance travelled
    C   the cost of oil and petrol
    D   the cost of garaging

40   If car hirers change their minds after paying the whole cost of hiring, the £12 booking fee is
    A   returned in part immediately.
    B   not returned at all.
    C   not required.
    D   returned in full within six weeks.

PAPER 2 COMPOSITION (1½ hours)

*Write **two only** of the following composition exercises. Your answers must follow exactly the instructions given and must be of between 120 and 180 words each.*

1   The radio-cassette recorder you bought recently is not working properly. Write the letter you would send with the recorder to the manufacturers, explaining the fault and asking them to repair it.

2   Imagine you are the mayor of your local town. Write a speech to welcome a group of foreign schoolchildren and their teachers who are visiting your town.

3   Describe a journey (by land, sea or air) on which you met a particularly unpleasant person.

4   'Much stricter punishments would soon reduce the amount of crime.' What is your opinion?

5   Based on your reading of any one of these books, write on *one* of the following.

    JANE AUSTEN: *Sense and Sensibility*
    'Mr Willoughby has not behaved as a gentleman should.' What had Willoughby done to make Elinor think so badly of him?

    G. B. SHAW: *Arms and the Man*
    What are Captain Bluntschli's views on war?

    GRAHAM GREENE: *The Third Man*
    What sort of man was Rollo Martins and why did he go to Vienna?

PAPER 3   USE OF ENGLISH   (2 hours)

1   *Fill each of the numbered blanks in the following passage. Use only **one** word in each space.*

The two women were standing now on the deck of the steamer looking at the riverside scene. To the left lay a .... (1) of small boats .... (2) the landing stage. Behind .... (3) the smooth white fronts of the hotels .... (4) above the yellow city walls. Straight ahead was .... (5) Ellie had brought her to .... (6): a line of flat boats with a wooden walkway laid .... (7) it, crowded at .... (8) evening hour .... (9) country people returning from market. This made .... (10) truly fascinating sight. They .... (11) see the brightly- .... (12) skirts of the women and the bundles on the backs of the men .... (13) they moved towards the .... (14) shore. Working .... (15) way against them was a .... (16) of soldiers coming down .... (17) the castle to spend the evening in the town. .... (18) a gun sounded from the bank .... (19) them both to start and hold .... (20) other's hands more tightly.

2   *Finish each of the following sentences in such a way that it means exactly the same as the sentence printed before it.*

> EXAMPLE: I haven't enjoyed myself so much for years.
>
> ANSWER: It's years *since I enjoyed myself so much.*

a)   I'm always nervous when I travel by air.

Travelling ....

b)   He could not afford to buy the car.

The car ....

c)   'Why don't you put your luggage under the seat?' he asked.

He suggested ....

d)   Although he had a good salary, he was unhappy in his job.

In spite ....

e)   He was annoyed because his secretary came late to work.

He objected ....

f)   I'm sorry I missed your birthday party.

I wish ....

g)   They haven't cleaned the streets this week.

The streets ....

h)   Apples are usually cheaper than oranges.

Apples are not ....

i)   I advise you to put your money in the bank.

You'd ....

j)   That restaurant is so dirty that no one wants to eat there.

It is such ....

3 *In each of the following sentences there is a blank with a word just before it. Fill each blank with a word that combines with the one given in a way that fits the sentence.*

EXAMPLE: He paid a lot of money for his first-*class* ticket.

a) She hasn't much money to spend because she can find only a part-

.... job.

b) John always wears very well- .... shoes.

c) He looks rather severe but he is really a very kind- .... man.

d) People often put on weight when they become middle- ....

e) My mother always gives her guests home- .... cakes for tea.

4 *Fill each blank with a phrase made from* **go**.

EXAMPLE: The price of petrol has *gone up* from 40p to 50p per litre.

a) You will have to .... your homework again because it's full of mistakes.

b) When the tide .... there's plenty of sand to sit on.

c) The milk smells horrible. It must have .... , so you will have to put lemon in your tea.

d) As two of the staff here have .... with flu, we can't finish the work today.

e) She swims so well that she really should .... the competition.

5 *In the following conversation, the parts numbered (1) to (6) have been left out. Complete them suitably.*

    A   Worldwide Travel Services—Can I help you?

    B   Yes, thank you. I would like to go to New York as soon as possible. When (1) .... ?

    A   There will be a flight tomorrow at 12.15.

    B   Are (2) .... ?

    A   Yes, Sir. The flight is not yet fully booked.

    B   What (3) .... ?

    A   A first-class single ticket is £315.

    B   Can (4) .... ?

    A   Certainly, Sir. Two first-class tickets for flight number CX202.

    B   When (5) .... ?

    A   If you come to my office after 4 p.m. today I will have them ready for you.

    B   Only one more thing. How (6) .... ?

    A   We can send a car to your hotel or you can reserve seats in our private coach.

6   The following four people are travelling on a train, reading different newspapers or magazines. Using the information given, continue paragraphs 1–4 on page 69 in about 50 words each.

Name	Age	Family	Job	Interests
Mary Brown	45	Married. 2 children, John (garage mechanic) Sandra (at Secretarial College).	Assistant in dress shop.	Making clothes for herself and daughter. Knitting. Collecting pictures of the Queen which she sticks into a book. Gossiping with friends about television and film stars.
James Moore	52	Married. 2 sons, both in family business.	Buying and selling houses.	Anything to do with making money. Owns large country house and likes buying things to make it more beautiful. Shooting and fishing.
Frank Smith	23	Single. Lives with parents in small town.	Railway clerk.	Football and swimming. Spends summer holidays in Spain and Portugal near hot, sandy beaches. Likes spending his evenings with his friends and going to discos.
Anne Jones	28	Recently married to a biologist.	College lecturer.	Playing the piano. Going to opera and concerts. Active member of local political group. Likes discussing woman's place in the modern world. Entertaining friends to dinner.

People's Daily	Economic News	MODERN SOCIETY	POPULAR OPINION
★Sandra's Friend the Elephant	Pound/Dollar—Latest fears	—Zambia-Progress Report	Royal Babies —delightful picture series
★Disco Beat Latest (Mick's new album)	Investment Advice	—Secretary or Career Woman?	On with the Old Love —Patricia explains
★Win your next great Mediterranean sun holiday	This week's special features on	—Chopin Festival	Fashion at your fingertips —useful ideas
★3 pages of Sports news	COUNTRY SPORTS ANTIQUE FURNITURE	—International Cookery Series— Part 14	

(1) *I think Mary Brown is reading* ....

....

....

....

(2) *James Moore has chosen* ....

....

....

....

(3) *Frank Smith prefers* ....

....

....

....

(4) *Anne Jones is the sort of woman who reads* ....

....

....

....

PAPER 4   LISTENING COMPREHENSION
(about 30 minutes)

FIRST PART   E.G.

Put a tick (✓) against the two men Mary Brown describes.

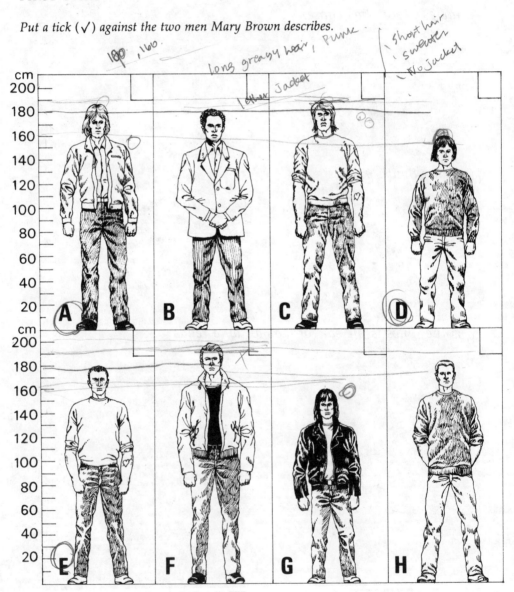

SECOND PART

For questions 2–14, fill in the missing information in the messages which Mrs Davis wrote for her husband after listening to the answering machine. The missing information you supply should be as brief as possible.

13th March

Mrs Curry (tel no ....8679.36.............................) ②
wants you to mend her .~~re pipe~~.............................. ③
water tap in bathroom.

Mr Harris rang.
He sounded slightly....~~nervous~~ annoyed................. ④
Can you go and mend his .~~heater~~ broken window~~s~~..... ⑤
Please either....~~Mrs 49 Gramsom cloth Vangal conor~~ ⑥
~~Go and see~~ him / call round / come round
OR ring his neighbour (tel no ..A69823.................) ⑦

Miss Embury rang to....applegize / say she is sorry ~~for~~ ⑧
not being there when you called.
Can you tell her how much it would cost....to paint her house ⑨
.... ? ⑨
Her tel no is....230980............................. ⑩

Mr Grant (tel no ....482984.............................) ⑪
                    ring
would like you to..~~repair central heating~~..........him ⑫
about his....Central heating / gas boiler............. ⑬
His address is ...64~~8~~ 7............Station Avenue. ⑭

THIRD PART

For questions 15–19 put a tick (√) in the box which corresponds to the man's answers.

15   Does he usually go abroad for summer holidays?

Yes	√
No	

16   Where did he go last year?

A	Italy	
B	Corfu	
C	Majorca	√
D	France	

17   How long did he go away for last year?

A	1 week	
B	2 weeks	
C	3 weeks	√

18   Where does he plan to go this year?

A	nowhere	
B	same place as last year	
C	not certain	√
D	Asia	√

19 Why does he say he will have a holiday this year?

A	He likes to get a suntan	
B	He likes to travel	
C	He deserves a holiday	✓
D	His friends have asked him	

For questions 20–22 tick the box which corresponds to the woman's answers.

20 Did she enjoy her holiday last year?

Yes	✓
No	

21 Where did she say she might go this year?

A	Italy	
B	France	
C	Greece	✓
D	Majorca	

22 How does she decide where to go on holiday?

A	friend's recommendation	
B	where the weather is good	
C	on a sudden idea	
D	by long-term planning	

Practice Test 4

PAPER 1   READING COMPREHENSION   (1 hour)

Answer all questions. Indicate your choice of answer in every case **on the separate answer sheet** *already given out, which should show your name and examination index number. Follow carefully the instructions about how to record your answers. Give* **one answer only** *to each question. Marks will not be deducted for wrong answers: your total score on this test will be the number of correct answers you give.*

SECTION A

In this section you must choose the word or phrase which best completes each sentence. **On your answer sheet** *indicate the letter A, B, C or D against the number of each item 1 to 25 for the word or phrase you choose.*

1 From the hotel there is a good .... of the mountains.
   A vision   B view   C sight   D picture

2 I'm sorry, I haven't got ....change. Why don't you try the bank?
   A some   B lots   C any   D all

3 If it .... fine, I shall go out.
   A was   B is   C were   D will be

4 We've .... of time to catch the train so there's no need to rush.
   A very much   B enough   C great deal   D plenty

5 I can't make .... what's happening.
   A away   B out   C do   D over

6 He's left his book at home; he's always so ....
   A forgetting   B forgotten   C forgettable   D forgetful

7 Driving a car with faulty brakes is .... quite a risk.
   A putting   B setting   C taking   D being

8 If we had known your new address, we .... to see you.
   A came   B will come   C would come   D would have come

9   A small .... of students was waiting outside the class to see the teacher.
     A gang   B crowd   C team   D group

10   Jenny and her sister are so ...., they could almost be twins.
     A likeness   B alike   C same   D the same

11   He went to Australia hoping to find a teaching .... without too much
     difficulty.
     A work   B occupation   C employment   D post

12   We'll play tennis and .... we'll have lunch.
     A then   B straight away   C immediately   D so

13   I hope he's .... to buy some bread; there's hardly any left.
     A reminded   B proposed   C suggested   D remembered

14   The accused man .... to give the police any more information.
     A objected   B denied   C refused   D disliked

15   Take the number 7 bus and get .... at Forest Road.
     A up   B down   C outside   D off

16   There is no .... in going to school if you're not willing to learn.
     A reason   B aim   C point   D purpose

17   She complained .... when she heard that she had to work on Sunday.
     A severely   B bitterly   C extremely   D terribly

18   For a long time after the accident, he suffered from constant .... in his back.
     A hurt   B ache   C pain   D injury

19   The policeman .... me the way.
     A told   B said   C explained   D directed

20   It was a very beautiful cloth .... from silk.
     A composed   B worn   C woven   D threaded

21   My mother was .... of making a cake when the front door bell rang.
     A at the centre   B on her way   C in the middle   D halfway through

22   .... you do better work than this, you won't pass the exam.
     A Although   B If   C Unless   D When

23   If you want to join the History Society, you must first .... this application
     form.
     A make up   B write down   C fill in   D do up   》》→

24   He has just taken an examination .... chemistry.
     A on   B about   C for   D in

25   The police have asked that .... who saw the accident should get in touch
     with them.
     A somebody   B someone   C one   D anyone

SECTION B

*In this section you will find after each of the passages a number of questions or unfinished
statements about the passage, each with four suggested answers or ways of finishing. You must
choose the one which you think fits best.* **On your answer sheet** *indicate the letter A, B, C or
D against the number of each item 26–40 for the answer you choose. Give one answer only to
each question. Read each passage right through before choosing your answers.*

FIRST PASSAGE

By far the most common snake in Britain is the adder. In Scotland, in fact, there are no
other snakes at all. The adder is also the only British snake with a poisonous bite. It can
be found almost anywhere, but prefers sunny hillsides and rough open country,
including high ground. In Ireland there are no snakes at all.

Most people regard snake bites as a fatal misfortune, but not all bites are serious,
and very few are fatal. Sometimes attempts at emergency treatment turn out to be
more dangerous than the bite itself, with amateurs heroically, but mistakenly, trying
do-it-yourself surgery and other unnecessary measures.

All snakes have small teeth, so it follows that all snakes can bite, but only the bite
of the adder presents any danger. British snakes are shy animals and are far more
frightened of you than you could possibly be of them. The adder will attack only if it
feels threatened, as can happen if you take it by surprise and step on it accidentally, or if
you try to catch it or pick it up, which it dislikes intensely. If it hears you coming, it will
normally get out of the way as quickly as it can, but adders cannot move very rapidly
and may attack before moving if you are very close.

The effect of a bite varies considerably. It depends upon several things, one of
which is the body-weight of the person bitten. The bigger the person, the less harmful
the bite is likely to be, which is why children suffer far more seriously from snake bites
than adults. A healthy person will also have better resistance against the poison.

Very few people actually die from snake bites in Britain, and though these bites
can make some people very ill, there are probably just as many cases of bites having
little or no effect, as there are of serious illness.

26 Adders are most likely to be found
    A   in wilder parts of Britain and Ireland.
    B   in Scotland and nowhere else.
    C   on uncultivated land throughout Britain.
    D   in shady fields in England.

27 If you are with someone who is bitten by an adder you should
    A   try to catch the adder.
    B   make no attempt to treat the bite.
    C   not worry about the victim.
    D   operate as soon as possible.

28 We are told that adders are
    A   normally friendly towards people.
    B   unlikely to bite except in self-defence.
    C   aggressive towards anyone in their territory.
    D   not afraid of human beings.

29 If an adder hears you approaching, it will usually
    A   move out of your path.
    B   take no notice of you at all.
    C   disappear very quickly.
    D   wait until you are close then attack.

30 We are told that in general British people think snakes are
    A   not very common in Britain.
    B   usually harmless.
    C   more dangerous than they usually are.
    D   unlikely to kill people by their bite.

SECOND PASSAGE

An industrial society, especially one as centralized and concentrated as that of Britain, is heavily dependent on certain essential services: for instance, electricity supply, water, rail and road transport, the harbours. The area of dependency has widened to include removing rubbish, hospital and ambulance services, and, as the economy develops, central computer and information services as well. If any of these services ceases to operate, the whole economic system is in danger.

It is this interdependency of the economic system which makes the power of trade unions such an important issue. Single trade unions have the ability to cut off many countries' economic blood supply. This can happen more easily in Britain than in some other countries, in part because the labour force is highly organized. About 55 per cent of British workers belong to unions, compared to under a quarter in the United States.

》》→

For historical reasons, Britain's unions have tended to develop along trade and occupational lines, rather than on an industry-by-industry basis, which makes a wages policy, democracy in industry and the improvement of procedures for fixing wage levels difficult to achieve.

There are considerable strains and tensions in the trade union movement, some of them arising from their outdated and inefficient structure. Some unions have lost many members because of industrial changes. Others are involved in arguments about who should represent workers in new trades. Unions for skilled trades are separate from general unions, which means that different levels of wages for certain jobs are often a source of bad feeling between unions. In traditional trades which are being pushed out of existence by advancing technologies, unions can fight for their members' disappearing jobs to the point where the jobs of other unions' members are threatened or destroyed. The printing of newspapers both in the United States and in Britain has frequently been halted by the efforts of printers to hold on to their traditional highly-paid jobs.

Trade unions have problems of internal communication just as managers in companies do, problems which multiply in very large unions or in those which bring workers in very different industries together into a single general union. Some trade union officials have to be re-elected regularly; others are elected, or even appointed, for life. Trade union officials have to work with a system of 'shop stewards' in many unions, 'shop stewards' being workers elected by other workers as their representatives at factory or works level.

31 Why is the question of trade union power important in Britain?
    A   The economy is very interdependent.
    B   Unions have been established a long time.
    C   There are more unions in Britain than elsewhere.
    D   There are many essential services.

32 Why is it difficult to improve the procedures for fixing wage levels?
    A   Some industries have no unions.
    B   Unions are not organized according to industries.
    C   Only 55 per cent of workers belong to unions.
    D   Some unions are too powerful.

33 Because of their out-of-date organization some unions find it difficult to
    A   change as industries change.
    B   get new members to join.
    C   learn new technologies.
    D   bargain for high enough wages.

34 Disagreements arise between unions because some of them
    A   try to win over members of other unions.
    B   ignore agreements.
    C   protect their own members at the expense of others.
    D   take over other unions' jobs.

35 In what ways are unions and large companies similar?
    A   Both have too many managers.
    B   Both have problems in passing on information.
    C   Both lose touch with individual workers.
    D   Both their managements are too powerful.

36 What basic problems are we told most trade unions face?
    A   They are not equal in size or influence.
    B   They are not organized efficiently.
    C   They are less powerful than employers' organizations.
    D   They do not have enough members.

THIRD PASSAGE

Breakaways

Short break holidays throughout Britain

Win A Super Value
Breakaway Weekend For 2

This is your chance to win a Breakaway weekend for two people at any of the 83 Breakaway hotels throughout Britain.

To win the Breakaway weekend for two, answer these four questions and send your entry, to arrive not later than 31 July 1985, to Team House, 24 Church Street, Ashford, Kent. TN25 5BJ.

---

1.   The St Vincent Rocks Hotel, Bristol is on the edge of the Avon Gorge which is crossed by the Clifton Bridge. Who designed the bridge?

2.   The Aerodrome Hotel, Croydon is next to the airfield from which England's famous solo pilot made her record flights in the 1930s. Who was she?

3.   The Talbot Hotel, Oundle, Northants is not far from the village of Fotheringay and the castle where one of history's most famous queens was imprisoned. Who was she?

4.   The Larkfield Hotel, Maidstone is a few miles away from one of England's top motor racing tracks. What is the name of the track?

The person whose correct entry is picked out first by a computer will win the prize. This decision is final. The winner will be sent a super value Breakaway booklet giving details of the 83 hotels from which he/she can choose where to spend the prize weekend.

Every Breakaway hotel gives you the chance to see something different, while providing you with comfortable surroundings and good food.

A Breakaway weekend includes a three-course dinner, accommodation and a full English breakfast, for two nights. You also get Sunday lunch, either a traditional meal at your hotel, or, if you are planning to go sightseeing, the hotel will provide a packed lunch for you.

Breakaway hotels are great places for families. Children can choose from their own special menu, and for those up to 12 years old accommodation is free of charge when sharing a room with their parents.

A super value Breakaway booklet will be sent to you if you contact this number: 0252 517517.

37 This competition will be won by the person
    A   who sends in the first correct answers.
    B   whose correct entry is selected by a computer.
    C   whose entry arrives first on 31 July.
    D   whose entry is the final one selected by the computer.

38 Question 4 in the competition is different from the others because
    A   the hotel described is a modern one.
    B   it asks about a place not a person.
    C   the hotel can be reached easily by car.
    D   the answer is the name of a man.

39 The winner's weekend will include
    A   a free room for children under 12.
    B   dinner on two days and one lunch.
    C   dinner and packed lunches on two days.
    D   light breakfasts in his/her room.

40 The advertisement suggests that the best way to get a Breakaway booklet is to
    A   enter the competition.
    B   write to one of the hotels.
    C   write to Team House.
    D   telephone 0252 517517.

PAPER 2   COMPOSITION   (1½ hours)

*Write **two only** of the following composition exercises. Your answers must follow exactly the instructions given and must be of between 120 and 180 words each.*

1 You have received an invitation to a friend's wedding, but it is impossible for you to accept it. Write a letter to your friend explaining this, and mentioning the present you are sending.

2 You have a job as a tourist guide, and you have to talk to groups of people about places or buildings in your city. Tell them about one particularly interesting place to visit.

3 'Thank God it was only a dream!' Write a story ending with these words.

4 Computers and other machines are becoming more and more important in everyday life. Do you welcome this trend, or dislike it?

5 Based on your reading of any one of these books, write on *one* of the following.

G. B. SHAW: *Arms and the Man*
'The soul of a servant'. Explain how this phrase is used in the play.

Outstanding Short Stories (LONGMAN)
Tell the story of Susan Bell as if you were Aaron Dunn *or* Kate O'Brien.

PETER DICKINSON: *The Seventh Raven*
Describe the 'opera mafia' and explain why it has this name.

PAPER 3   USE OF ENGLISH   (2 hours)

1   *Fill each of the numbered blanks in the following passage. Use only* **one** *word in each space.*

I used to go into the countryside to sketch animals and plants, carrying my drawing materials in a bag. One day I was walking across a field, looking .... (1) rabbits to draw. Lost .... (2) thought, I .... (3) not noticed a bull running towards me. About one hundred metres .... (4) was a tree under .... (5) I intended to sit and draw. Suddenly, I .... (6) a noise behind me. I turned and saw the bull. I knew that a bull can run .... (7) faster .... (8) a man, but I also knew that a bull cannot see very .... (9) and notices only shape and movement. I .... (10) not panic but ran towards the tree, keeping the .... (11), myself and the bull in a straight line. To distract the bull, I then threw my bag to the right, so it was out of the line of the tree. The bull saw .... (12) sudden movement and headed towards the bag. I .... (13) the tree and climbed up it. From .... (14) I watched the bull attacking my bag with its horns and feet. It continued to .... (15) this for fifteen minutes and I was very .... (16) to be up the tree. .... (17), the bull was satisfied and moved off. I waited until it was a very long way .... (18) and then got down from the tree and picked up my bag. I left the field as fast as I .... (19) and then looked inside my bag. Everything in it was .... (20) ruined.

2   *Finish each of the following sentences in such a way that it means exactly the same as the sentence printed before it.*

EXAMPLE: I haven't enjoyed myself so much for years.

ANSWER: It's years   *since I enjoyed myself so much.*

a)   Unless he phones immediately he won't get any information.

If ....

b)   How long is it since they bought the house?

When ....

c)   He couldn't repair the broken vase.

The ....

d)   The garden still needs digging.

The garden hasn't ....

e)   Have you got a cheaper carpet than this?

Is this ....

f)   I can't get my feet into these shoes.

These shoes ....

g)   I am very pleased that we shall meet again soon.

I am looking ....

h)   'Keep away from this area,' said the security guard, when we approached the fence.

The security guard told ....

i)   I've never met such a famous person before.

It's ....

j)   This pudding can be cooked in its tin.

You don't ....

3 *Complete the following sentences by writing in the space provided a suitable word meaning the opposite of the word in capital letters.*

EXAMPLE: Cinderella was very BEAUTIFUL, but both her sisters were very *ugly*.

a) Although the earlier scientific experiments had been FAILURES this one was a complete ....

b) The first eight battles fought by the General resulted in his DEFEAT, so his final .... surprised everyone.

c) He was not sure if turning the screw to the left would TIGHTEN it or .... it.

d) Make sure the bread you buy is .... not STALE.

e) The water in the tank always FREEZES at night but the ice soon .... when the sun comes up.

4 *Complete the following sentences with an expression formed from* **put**.

EXAMPLE: You must *put out* the lights before you leave.

a) That man is so rude I just can't ....
his behaviour any longer.

b) Because she kept .... going to the dentist, her toothache got worse.

c) You are .... weight. You'll have to stop eating chocolate.

d) Look at this mess! .... your toys .... at once.

5   *Complete the following dialogue.*

(In the Tourist Information Office, Avebury, Wiltshire, England.)

Tourist: Are there any interesting walks we can take in the countryside in this area?

Officer: Oh yes, there's the 'Ridgeway Path'. It's a very popular place to walk.

Tourist: (1) .... ?

Officer: 150 kilometres. It's one of our long-distance footpaths.

Tourist: (2) .... !

Officer: Oh, you don't have to walk all of it. You can do just a part.

Tourist: (3) .... ?

Officer: No, ordinary shoes will do, at this time of year anyway. Of course, you shouldn't wear high-heels or anything like that.

Tourist: (4) .... ?

Officer: No, I'm sure that won't happen. The path is easy to follow and there are plenty of signs.

Tourist: (5) .... ?

Officer: Lots of interesting historical and archaeological sites, and some marvellous views from the hills. We believe the path is over 5,000 years old. We have a map and a guide-book which explain all about it.

Tourist: (6) .... ?

Officer: The map is 80p and the guide-book is £1.50p.

Tourist: (7) ....

Officer: Here you are. That will be £2.30p, please.

6 *Study the illustration showing the cost and journey time of different ways of travelling from London to Manchester, and the notes below. Complete the paragraphs on page 88 in the spaces provided, explaining which way you think each person should travel in winter when the weather is bad. (You may choose any way for any person, provided you give reasons.)*

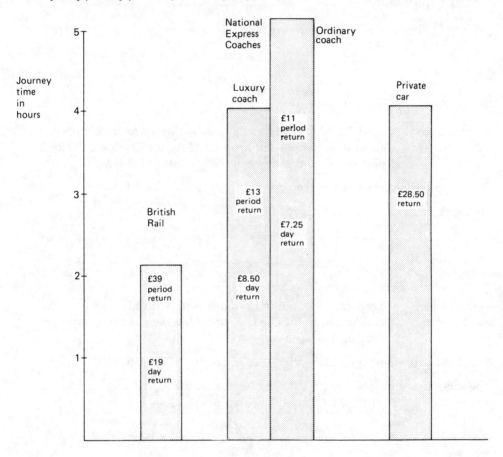

London – Manchester: journey times and fares.

Notes

1. Day return ticket – you must go and come back the same day.

2. Period return ticket – you can go and come back up to three months later.

3. Luxury coaches have reclining seats, toilets, food and drink, hostesses, and video films. Ordinary coaches have none of these.

4. The cost of the car journey includes all the costs of running a car, not just petrol costs.

5. Students and children can get reductions on trains but not on coaches.

Philip Smith   aged 23. He needs to go to Manchester, where he has never been before, for an interview for a new job and must be there by 10 a.m. All his expenses will be paid by the the company. He has a car.

I think Philip Smith will go by .... (Cost £   )

because ....

....

....

....

Agnes Clark   aged 72. She needs to go to Manchester to look after her sister who has just left hospital. If Agnes sits down for long periods of time, she gets terrible pains in her legs.

In my opinion Agnes Clark will go by .... (Cost £   )

because ....

....

....

....

James Norris   aged 42. He is going to Manchester with his wife and two children to spend the Christmas holiday, as usual, with his parents. He has a car.

It would be best for James to travel by .... (Cost £   )

because ....

....

....

....

Mary Stevens   aged 22. She is going to Manchester to spend the weekend with her boyfriend and his family. She was a student at London University and has just started her first job. She hasn't got a car.

I believe Mary Stevens will choose to go by .... (Cost £   )

because ....

....

....

....

PAPER 4   LISTENING COMPREHENSION
(about 30 minutes)

FIRST PART

For questions 1–4 tick (√) one of the boxes A, B, C or D.

1   Lona spent her childhood

A   in North Carolina.

B   on a dairy farm.

C   in Florida.

D   on the West Coast.

A	
B	
C	
D	

2   Lona likes reading about

A   sewing.

B   science fiction.

C   history.

D   travel.

A	
B	
C	
D	

3   Lona and her family have

A   spent holidays in Austria.

B   been on trips to Virginia.

C   spent holidays in the U.K.

D   been on trips to the West Coast.

A	
B	
C	
D	

4   Living where she does Lona misses

A   winter sports.

B   seasonal changes.

C   snow and ice.

D   water sports.

A	
B	
C	
D	

SECOND PART

Listen to the conversation between the old lady and her neighbour, and then fill in the spaces in this note. Be as brief as possible.

What to do while the old lady is away!

5. She'll be back on _____.

6. Tins of cat food _____ the fridge.

7. Give the cat _____ tin(s) each day.

8. Water the garden if_____.

9. Water the tomatoes_____.

10. Water the houseplants _____.

11. Leave the _____ on sometimes.

12. Her phone number while she's away will

     be _____.

THIRD PART

For questions 13–20 tick (√) whether the statements are true or false.

		True	False
13	Suggestions are given on what to do both in and around the city.	V	
14	The zoo is open every day of the year.	V	~~√~~
15	Buses take 50 minutes to reach the zoo.	~~√~~	V
16	A dancing display will take place at the Ross Open Air Theatre.	V	
17	Refreshments are available in Duddingston Church in the afternoon.	√	
18	Coach tours of the city start from St Andrew's Square.		V
19	The Camera Obscura should be visited at night.		√
20	An orchestral concert will take place in the King's Theatre this evening.	~~√~~	√

FOURTH PART

Listen to this conversation between two people who work in a hospital and have to provide equipment for the nurses' training programme; fill in the details in the diary.

Fill in the gaps 21–23 on the page from the diary shown below.

---

29 Thursday

> *Health Centre*
>
> *in Lecture Theatre*
>
> *requires TV*

30 Friday

> ㉑ .... *Foundation*
>
> ㉒ *in* ....
>
> ㉓ *requires projector and* ....

1 Saturday

> *In-service training*
>
> *in Lecture Theatre*
>
> *requires mic. + speakers.*

PART THREE   The Key

Key to Practice Test 1

PAPER 1   READING COMPREHENSION

SECTION A

(See *Study Notes p. 8 for Suggested method of working.*)

1   D   *a check-up*
Meaning: Your doctor should regularly check your general health.
Distractor check:
A   *a revision*   These regulations need a thorough revision.
B   *a control*   You can adjust the brightness of the television picture by using a control at the back of the set.
C   *an investigation*   The police started an investigation as soon as the theft was reported.

2   C   *persuade*†
Meaning: You can't make me change my plans.
Distractor check:
A   *convince*   You cannot convince me that you are right.
B   *impress*   You don't impress me with all your boasting.
D   *urge*   I urge you to think very carefully before making such an important decision.

3   D   *crop*
Meaning: The farm will probably produce more potatoes this year.
Distractor check:
A   *product*   The factory's most successful product is an electric can-opener.
B   *outcome*   At this stage in the negotiations, it is too early to suggest what the outcome may be.
C   *amount*   The amount of butter produced depends on the quality of the milk used.

4   C   *quite*
Meaning: She was fairly helpful.
Distractor check:

† This is correct because it fits the structure of the sentence as well as the meaning.

A   *entirely*   I'm not entirely sure what you mean. Could you explain again please?
B   *exactly*   Copy the words on the card exactly. Make no changes.
D   *totally*   You look totally different without your glasses!
(note: in these contexts 'totally' and 'entirely' are both appropriate)

5 A   *signal*
Meaning: He made a sound or movement to tell them when to start.
Distractor check:
B   *warning*   Without any warning, the lights all went out.
C   *shot*   The policeman fired a shot in the air to summon help.
D   *show*   We didn't really want to listen to him, but we put on a show of interest, out of politeness.

6 C   *shame*
Meaning: I regret very much that your wife wasn't able to come.
Distractor check:
A   *harm*   Careless use of chemicals often does great harm to the environment.
B   *sorrow*   It was with great sorrow that we heard of the death of your son.
D   *shock*   The news of the disaster was a terrible shock.

7 C   *Apart*†
Meaning: Bill didn't want to go, but all the other students did.
Distractor check:
A   *Except*   They all wanted to go except for Bill.
B   *Only*   Bill was the only student who didn't want to go.
D   *Separate*   Bill is making separate travel arrangements as he doesn't like flying.

8 B   *establish*
Meaning: She intends to set up a new system within the company.
Distractor check:
A   *manufacture*   In this workshop we manufacture soft toys.
C   *control*   We control the quality of our products by means of frequent checks.
D   *restore*   The new tax regulations are too complicated to administer, so the government has decided to restore the old ones.

9 B   *adjust*
Meaning: Don't try to improve the picture by altering the controls on your television set because the problem is at the TV station.
Distractor check:

† This is correct because it fits the structure of the sentence as well as the meaning.

A   *change*   We can't fix this television: you'll have to change it for a new one.
C   *repair*   My television isn't working, so I've got to call someone in to repair it.
D   *switch*   The play was so boring I decided to switch over to the other channel.

10   B   *influential*
Meaning: He changed the way people thought about certain subjects.
Distractor check:
A   *ordinary*   Most of the stories in this book are quite ordinary, only the last one is a bit special.
C   *unlimited*   The range of goods on sale is so great that one's choice is almost unlimited.
D   *accurate*   Before drawing your plan make sure that the measurements are accurate.

11   B   *delicious*
Meaning: The pears were very tasty.
Distractor check:
A   *flavoured*   The rice was flavoured with saffron.
C   *tasteful*   The room was decorated in an elegant, tasteful manner.
D   *desirable*   It is neither convenient nor desirable for the managing director to visit Spain this spring.

12   D   *dismissed†*
Meaning: They will be asked to leave their jobs.
Distractor check:
A   *refused*   I refused to give him a job because he didn't have the right qualifications.
B   *rejected*   Several applications were rejected by the company because the forms were incorrectly filled in.
C   *disapproved*   We disapproved of his behaviour but there was nothing we could do about it.

13   C   *charge†*
Meaning: He was responsible for organizing and controlling them.
Distractor check:
A   *management*   He started as a shop floor worker, but now he is in management and doing very well.
B   *leadership*   The leadership of the party must listen to the opinions of all the members.
D   *direction*   The actors were very enthusiastic, but the play was not a success, because of poor direction.

† This is correct because it fits the structure of the sentence as well as the meaning.

14   C   *There*†
Meaning: The speaker is pointing to the bus as it disappears up the road.
Distractor check:
A   *On time*   My train arrived on time, so I wasn't late for the meeting.
B   *At once*   We must leave at once, there is no time to spare.
D   *Early*   You will have to arrive early if you want to reserve a seat.

15   D   *presented*†
Meaning: They gave him a clock as an official gift from the company.
Distractor check:
A   *offered*   He was offered a part-time job, but he refused it.
B   *pleased*   He was very pleased with his present.
C   *satisfied*   We are most satisfied with your work and would like to offer you a salary increase.

16   B   *behind*
Meaning: He couldn't take his family with him. He left them at home.
Distractor check:
A   *at a loss*   I am at a loss to understand you. What are you talking about?
C   *out*   If any of the questions are too difficult, leave them out and I'll explain them later.
D   *at all costs*   However bad the weather, the roads must be kept open at all costs.

17   D   *interested*†
Meaning: Your information interests me very much.
Distractor check:
A   *concerned*   I am very concerned about my sister. She has never been out this late before.
B   *surprised*   I was very surprised by the announcement of their marriage.
C   *interesting*   I'm reading a very interesting book about the history of medicine.

18   B   *spare*†
Meaning: He only had a few minutes free.
Distractor check:
A   *provide*   The manager said he would provide me with all the materials I needed for the job.
C   *hear*   He couldn't hear what I said because the machines were making so much noise.
D   *let*   He let the children stay in the room while he worked, provided they were quiet.

---

† This is correct because it fits the structure of the sentence as well as the meaning.

19 B   *after*
Meaning: I chased him.
Distractor check:
A   *into*   By chance I ran into one of my former students at the theatre last week and had a long chat with her.
C   *over*   When he saw the road accident, the farmer ran over from his barn to offer help as quickly as he could.
(note: the most usual meaning of 'run over' is to 'drive your car over' something, crushing it)
D   *near*   They were very frightened when the child ran near the road and were more careful after that.

20 A   *put off*
Meaning: The match will be postponed till Saturday.
Distractor check:
B   *cancel*   We had to cancel the match because several players were ill and no one was free at a later date.
C   *play*   We can play next Saturday if everyone is free.
D   *put away*   When you have finished your game, please put away all the equipment.

21 A   *lend*
Meaning: When you let someone use one of your possessions for a limited time, there is a possibility that it may not be returned to you.
Distractor check:
B   *offer*   If he hasn't got a car, can you offer him a lift to the station?
C   *borrow*   May I borrow your pen? I've forgotten to bring one with me.
D   *lose*   If you lose your passport, contact the police immediately.

22 D   *bothering*†
Meaning: He didn't take the trouble to read the address.
Distractor check:
A   *worrying*   Worrying about your exams won't help you to pass them.
B   *caring*   Caring for the elderly can be very rewarding work.
C   *fearing*   Fearing a thunderstorm, we moved the exhibits indoors.

23 A   *held up*†
Meaning: The traffic was delayed because of the hole in the road.
Distractor check:
B   *kept down*   The company kept down costs by buying cheaper raw materials.
C   *stood back*   We stood back from the road to avoid being splashed by passing vehicles.
D   *sent back*   When they reached the frontier they were sent back because their passports were out of date.

† This is correct because it fits the structure of the sentence as well as the meaning.

24 B *swept*†
Meaning: The current carried him along, against his will.
Distractor check:
A *caught* As soon as the athletes arrived, they were caught up in a round of entertainments.
C *thrown* She was thrown off her horse during the race and seriously injured.
D *swung* The troop of soldiers swung out of the gate and marched up the road.

25 A *lost*†
Meaning: The ship sank and nobody saw any sign of it after the storm.
Distractor check:
B *crashed* The car crashed into the wall.
C *disappeared* The old ship disappeared and was never seen again.
D *vanished* The ship vanished in the mist.

SECTION B

FIRST PASSAGE

26 A
because
It was a very ordinary place. (paragraphs 1 and 2)
Distractor check:
B She had visited it often as a child.
C Only when her grandmother died, according to the text.
D Maybe, but this would not affect her memories.

27 D
because
It was about 6 miles out. (paragraph 2, lines 1–3)
Distractor check:
A It was further than that.
B It was a bus ride away!
C Her grandparents depended partly on 'the shop in the nearest village'.

28 B
because
'EEL' above the door were probably the builder's or original owner's. (paragraph 3, lines 7–9)
Distractor check:
A There is no suggestion of this.

† This is correct because it fits the structure of the sentence as well as the meaning.

C   'EEL' might have been his initials, 'name' is not suggested.
D   It was Frances who didn't know why.

29 C
    because
    'The place had come to depress her.' (paragraph 1, line 5)
    Distractor check:
    A   There is no evidence of this in the passage.
    B   Her grandmother was difficult, but no major quarrels are mentioned.
    D   Only with her grandmother.

30 C
    because
    'It had been the one fixed point in her childhood.' (paragraph 3, lines 1–2)
    Distractor check:
    A   She was brought up by her parents, not her grandparents.
    B   There is no evidence of this in the passage.
    D   There is no evidence of this in the passage.

SECOND PASSAGE

31 B
    because
    This will make sure 'that trees have a desired shape'. (paragraph 2, line 1)
    Distractor check:
    A   Pruning is used to get it to the right height, not necessarily taller.
    C   The opposite is true: it is to help small branches grow.
    D   Pruning may thicken the whole tree's appearance, not the small
        branches.

32 A
    because
    They can 'prevent the free movement of air'. (paragraph 2, line 7)
    Distractor check:
    B   Wind is not mentioned.
    C   There is no evidence of this in the passage.
    D   They are only mentioned in connection with appearance.

33 B
    because
    A wound 'provides an easy entry for disease'. (paragraph 3, lines 1–2)
    Distractor check:
    A   You do this *before* painting the tree.
    C   You shouldn't use it on a rough surface.
    D   You wait until the wound is dry before you paint it.

34 C
because
You shouldn't prune too often or for no good reason.
Distractor check:
A   The text says winter is best.
B   There is no evidence of this in the passage.
D   This would probably be too often. 'Regularly' is not specified in the passage.

35 B
because
It talks about reasons, results and problems.
Distractor check:
A   It only gives instructions for protecting the tree after pruning, it doesn't tell you *how to prune*, what tools to use, etc.
C   This is not the main topic.
D   It doesn't discuss any methods of pruning.

PASSAGE THREE

36 C
because
It has the feel of comedy about it, especially in the sentence about growing a moustache. (line 5)
Distractor check:
A   This is a serious historical novel.
B   This is an 'exact record' of life in a 'world of work and poverty', so there will be little humour.
D   This sounds rather depressing; the man's life is described as empty and he has a terrible secret.

37 D
because
Nothing in the description suggests the past.
Distractor check:
A   This is set in Ancient Rome.
B   This is set 'at the end of the last century', that is, the nineteenth century.
C   This is set in the early 20th century, when 'the first motor buses' were used.

38 C
because
He conquered Britain. (lines 7–8)
Distractor check:

A   His actions are 'far from foolish'.
B   He became Emperor 'reluctantly'.
D   What about 'his final hard judgement' on his wife?

39   A
because
University research is mentioned, and he is present at the opening of an
important historical grave.
Distractor check:
B   The reference to 'university research' sounds a bit academic for that.
C   There is no evidence for this.
D   There is no specific information about age and he was present when
    the grave was opened years ago.

40   C
because
Johnson supported him 'in moments of difficulty'. (lines 5–6)
Distractor check:
A   We don't know this.
B   On the contrary, the text implies that he probably did, if Cecil needed
    his approval to grow a moustache.
D   There is no evidence of this in the passage.

PAPER 2   COMPOSITION

NOTES

(These notes may be consulted at various stages in your work. See Study Notes, p. 11.)

1

Task Check
You must remember – you are in London
                  – you have been there one month (so this is probably not
                    your first letter!)
You must mention – information about the course
                  – difficulties (they needn't all be connected with your
                    studies)

Register Check
Informal

Technique
If you haven't written this sort of letter for a while, check in a reference book the rules for setting out informal letters. Don't begin 'Dear My Parents'. This is bad grammar as well as bad style. You can use the names you usually call them, or better still, use English: 'Dear Mum and Dad' or 'Dear Father and Mother' are quite acceptable. Choose the ones which seem comfortable to you.

DANGER! Don't turn it into a letter of complaint. Put some good points in as well. Remember to describe the course generally, as well as mentioning your difficulties.

Sample Plan

para 1 - thanks for their last letter; news of the family
para 2 - the course, routine (times, teachers, homework, special lessons)
para 3 - problems experienced:
    understanding the teacher
    not used to working in the afternoon
    traffic jams and crowded buses
para 4 - managing OK in spite of problems described
    - don't worry
    - love to all

2

Task Check
You must mention – what's wrong with the food
                – what's wrong with the service
                – suggestions for improvements

Register Check
This is direct speech, so use speech forms (for example, 'doesn't' for 'does not'), but remember to be fairly formal so that you sound respectful and polite.

Technique
Think about the sort of language you need when representing other people, for example, 'on behalf of'.

Check forms used for making <u>suggestions</u>, for example, 'would it be possible . . .?' 'we wondered whether you could . . .'

DANGER! Don't get so carried away with your complaints that you leave no time for suggestions.

Sample Plan

para 1 – thanks for agreeing to listen
para 2 – problems a) food: not enough hot food
b) service : kitchen staff impatient,
sometimes rude
para 3 – cause : staff shortage, no time to cook and clear up
para 4 – suggestion : students can clear tables, so staff have
more time for cooking
para 5 – hope suggestion accepted

3

Task Check
This must be a first-person narrative about a fire.

Register Check
It can be informal.

Technique
Plan very carefully, think about how your story will end before you begin to write. Make a list of key words and phrases. Make the style interesting and varied by, for example, using short and long sentences and some direct speech. Revise punctuation of direct speech.

DANGER! Don't lose control of language in the excitement of making a good story. Don't start sentences you can't complete: for example, if you don't know the word 'stretcher', don't start a sentence 'The ambulance men lifted him onto a . . .' Instead, write 'The ambulance men lifted him gently and carried him to . . .'

Sample Plan

para 1 – Fire! First think it's a joke. Then open door, smoke
         coming up.
para 2 – Say, must get out. Wake baby. Wet towels over heads.
para 3 – Going down. Friends carrying baby, self last.
         Dark, heat, smoke, can't breathe, nearly falling.
para 4 – Suddenly fresh air, safety. Never joke about
         fire alarm again.

Example words and phrases:
         it's someone fooling about
         billowing smoke
         don't panic
         to feel one's way
         to choke
         relief

4

Task Check
You must suggest at least one solution for youth unemployment. Remember to
answer the question about traditional ideas about work.

Register Check
Use fairly formal language to match this serious question.

Technique
It doesn't matter what opinions you have, provided that they are developed
logically and expressed in accurate English. Give some concrete examples to
illustrate your ideas.

DANGER! Plan carefully – muddled ideas produce muddled language!

> **Sample Plan**
>
> *para 1 – reasons: one major cause of unemployment – people not trained for jobs available (e.g. unemployed mechanic, shortage of electricians)*
>
> *para 2 – solutions: schools, colleges must keep in touch with industry – be up-to-date (e.g. secretaries must have word processor skills, not just traditional typing, etc.)*
>
> *para 3 – solutions: unemployed must try to be flexible and older people change traditional ideas – re-training to move from old industries to new*
>
> *para 4 – government must help unemployed to find jobs by organizing proper training for all age groups*

PAPER 3   USE OF ENGLISH

Question 1

1   him
2   for
3   after
4   cycled/rode/pedalled
5   bridge/first
6   at/by/past/near/towards
7   in/on/off
8   bought/taken/purchased
9   could
10 or
11 telephoned/rung/phoned/called/contacted
12 slightly/working/back
13 to
14 unlocked/opened
15 once
16 been
17 no
18 since
19 to
20 would

Common error check:

4   went ✗
This is the word we use for the *whole* journey. In this sentence the reader's attention is drawn to *how* he did the last part.

14   reached ✗
This would mean that either a) the door was already open so he would *already* be able to see into the hall or b) the door was still shut so he *couldn't* see into the hall!

18   when ✗
'when they returned' is a point in time, so he couldn't *always* have known something would happen. The time *since*, on the other hand, is a period of time, so it is possible he knew something throughout that period, or 'always'.

Question 2

a) John suggested | *(that) Barry (should) put* / *to Barry (that) he (should) put* | a better lock on the door.

b) Despite his | *(two) broken legs* / *legs both being broken* | in the crash, he managed to get out of the car before it exploded.

c) This is the first | *time* | *I have eaten* | this kind of food.

d) The firemen managed | *to put the fire out* / *to put out the fire* | after fighting it for twelve hours.

e) Plans | *have* | *been drawn (up)* | for an extension to the house.

f) We saw the house in Stratford-on-Avon | *where* / *in which* | Shakespeare was born.

g) You | *don't need* / *don't have* / *need not* / *needn't* | *to finish* / *to finish* / *finish* / *finish* | by Saturday.

h) The journalist wanted to know | *how many survivors there were.* / *the number of survivors.*

i) The meat was | *so rotten that* | it had to be thrown away.

j) Professor Van Helsing | *must* / *has to* | *be met* | at the airport.

Question 3

a) cash
b) exchange
c) discount
d) loan/overdraft
e) interest

Question 4

a) down
b) away
c) out
d) (a)round
e) on

Question 5

a) I was very surprised | at / by | the | letter that | I received | from you | this morning.

b) In it | you say / it says | I have not paid | for / a | the | book | you sent | me one month ago.

c) You say | I must send / I have to send / I should send | you | the money / some money | immediately.

d) In fact | I returned | the book | to you | the same day | I received it.

e) I did not return it | because | I did not want it.

f) But because | the book | was | in (a) poor condition | with several torn pages.

g) I sent | you | a letter | at the time / at that time | asking you / and asked you / to ask you | to send | me | a perfect copy | of | the same book.

h) I hope that | you will do that | and that | I will not have | to write | to you | again | about this matter.

Question 6

Step one

Identify the three proposals.
These are underlined and numbered 1, 2 and 3 on the sample pages (pp. 110–11). 〰〰〰〰

Step two

Make notes.

Notes

1 — sold, demolished, new shopping centre built
2 — renovated inside, used for offices / social
    clubs, etc.
3 — front kept, everything else demolished
    new shopping centre built behind old fr.

Step three

Write the three sentences.
(See the sample pages.)

Step four

Find reasons for my choice.
These are highlighted on the sample pages.
Note: As this is an *opinion*, you may have a different answer, but you must be able to give logical reasons for it, using the information given.

Step five

Make notes.

My opinion

—compromise (architect's)

— perfect e.g. of C17th style   *BUT* terrible state inside

—jobs

— economic benefit *AND*   Keep only building
                             worth visiting

NB support growing

Step six

Write the paragraph.
(See the sample pages.)

PAPER 4: LISTENING COMPREHENSION

FIRST PART

Talking about study habits

1			✓
2	✓	✓	
3	✓		
4		✓	
5			
6			
7	✓		
8			

SAMPLE PAGE (see p. 108)

6   *Read the following passages about some proposed property developments in the town of Melchester, and look also at the instructions on page 33.*

From 'An Architectural Guide to Britain':

MELCHESTER (pop. 65,000)
The town is attractively situated on the River Ouse and dates from the ninth century. Despite its great age the town has few buildings of interest. In the last ten years there has been a lot of 'development' – new Town Hall, library, bus station, railway station. Perhaps the only building in the town which the visitor should make a point of seeing is the Old Grammar School. Built in the early seventeenth century by a rich local merchant, Sir William Waller, it is one of the oldest school buildings in England and is a perfect example of the style of that period. There is a magnificent exterior and inside some fine ceilings and panelled walls.

From the 'Melchester Times':

OLD SCHOOL TO MOVE TO NEW SITE

MR DAVID WALLER, Chairman of the Governors of the Old Grammar School has announced that a new school will be built on the outskirts of Melchester. To raise money for this the Old Grammar School is to be sold. The school is on a prime site in the centre of town. It may look beautiful from the outside but inside it is in a terrible state. It is dark and gloomy and there is little fresh air or light. It is more suitable for rabbits than schoolboys. It is costing us too much to keep on repairing it'. He added that Mega Properties had made a 'substantial offer' for the site.   ①

MEMO: URGENT

FROM: Lord Grabbit, Chairman of Mega Properties

TO: Peter Smooth, Publicity Officer, Mega
            Properties

   Apparently certain people in Melchester are
opposed to our plans to demolish the Old Grammar   ①
School and build a new shopping centre on the site
and are calling for the Minister of the Environment
to hold an inquiry. Please prepare some publicity
material to be sent to local newspapers and influential local people in the town. Point out that
both the construction of the centre and the shops
themselves will provide jobs for the people of
Melchester where there is a lot of unemployment.
Explain that the interior of the school is in such
a poor state that it cannot be used for any purpose.
The site is too important to have an empty or underused building on it and more people will come to
shop in the shopping centre than come to look at
the school.

To the editor of the 'Melchester Times':

Dear Sir,
   We are very disturbed by reports that the Old Grammar School is to be demolished by Mega Properties. Our town has already lost many of its historic old buildings which have been replaced by boring examples of modern architecture (several of them built by Mega Properties). The Old Grammar School is a building of great historical and architectural significance – to destroy it would be an act of vandalism. We are in favour of keeping the building and renovating the interior which could be used for offices, evening classes, exhibitions, a meeting place for local clubs and societies and many other purposes.   ②
Yours faithfully,

JOHN KEEP,
Chairman,
Melchester
Heritage Society

SAMPLE PAGE

To the editor of the
'Melchester Times':

Dear Sir,
I have been following with great interest the debate in your columns between those who wish to keep the Old Grammar School and those who wish to see a new shopping centre on the site. May I suggest a 'compromise'? Most people seem to agree that it is the exterior of the building which is beautiful. Why not keep the exterior frontage and build a shopping centre behind it, demolishing only the interior of the school? That way we could have the shopping centre and the best part of the school. As an architect, I know that this can be done.
Yours faithfully,
JOHN NASH

③

MEMO:

FROM: Lord Grabbit

TO: Peter Smooth

Support seems to be growing for the idea of keeping the exterior of the Old Grammar School. Attack this idea vigorously! It will be far cheaper and more convenient for us to demolish the entire school and start building on an empty site.

There are three proposals concerning the future of the Old Grammar School at Melchester. Describe each one in one sentence.

1 The Old Grammar School should be sold so that it can be demolished and replaced by a new shopping centre.

2 It should be renovated and preserved for use as offices or for various social activities.

3 Everything except the front wall should be demolished, so that a new shopping centre can be built behind the old frontage.

Which do you think is the best proposal? Complete the following paragraph in not more than 100 words, giving reasons for the one you have chosen and taking into account its advantages and disadvantages.

I think the best proposal is to follow the suggestion of the architect. The building is a perfect example of early seventeenth century style, but inside it is in a terrible state. Therefore, it would make sense to preserve only the exterior frontage. The new shopping centre will offer badly-needed jobs so Melchester will benefit economically without losing its only beautiful building. This proposal has the support of a growing number of local people, which is also very important.

SECOND PART

'Tell All' – a radio programme

9 false	15 false
10 true	16 false
11 true	17 true
12 true	18 true
13 true	19 false
14 true	20 false

THIRD PART

A cinema announcement
21 3.30
22 £1.10
23 First Love
24 2.15
25 Friday

FOURTH PART

A radio announcement
26 true
27 false
28 true
29 false
30 true

TAPESCRIPT

The rubric on this cassette follows exactly the wording of the Cambridge First Certificate Exam. To save space on the cassette the repeats have not been included. At the beginning of each passage, set the counter on your cassette player to zero. At the end of the passage, rewind the cassette to zero to hear the passage again. **Remember, you should hear each passage twice only!**

Cambridge First Certificate Listening Test

TEST NUMBER 1

You will be given a question paper for First Certificate Test 1. Your supervisor will give you further instructions. On the question paper you will see spaces for your name and index number, and questions for each part of the test. Each part of the test will be heard twice. There will be pauses to allow you to look through the questions before each part, and other pauses to let you think about your answers. At the end of every pause you will hear this sound.

tone

The tape will now be stopped while question papers are given out. You must ask any questions now, as you will not be allowed to speak during the test.

pause

First Part
You will hear two teachers in a staffroom discussing how they used to study when they were at university. For questions 1 to 8, tick the appropriate boxes.

pause

tone

★TONE★ Set the counter on your cassette player to zero now.

STUDY HABITS

Man: Do you find that you get a lot of students asking you for advice about revision techniques?

Woman: Well, yes, I mean, they do, but, when they've got quite big exams coming up, (*Yeah*), you know I really sort of find it quite a problem because you know, well I don't have to revise myself very often these days, and, but when I was at university, erm I mean, well, it just seems to be a matter of what suits one person doesn't suit another. (*Oh, yeah*) I mean, because, well, the girl I shared a house with at university. Now she worked, erm, she used to get up amazingly late, and, er, well, she didn't really start work until, er, in the evening I think, and, then she liked to have rock music on really loud and she used to, you know, play records really loud right through until sort of very late at night, you know, into the

Q1

113

small hours (*Oh God!*) and I was, sort of, well I was
just the opposite and er, well, the only way *I* could
ever get any work done was to make myself wake up
incredibly early and well, then work a bit and then ⎤ Q2
have some breakfast and, then, well, you know, I'd
sort of potter about a bit and then I'd go and do my
shopping and things, well that'd be sort of getting on
towards midday, but then in the afternoon I'd have a ⎤ Q7
rest and when I woke up I'd be thinking about eating
and I suppose I'd call that my supper, but, er, I mean
she was, it was her lunch or even you know brunch
that she was having at that time.

Man: Yeah, yeah, I suppose I'm a bit like you really. I like
to get up fairly early, say around seven, might have a
cup of coffee, and before I started get myself totally
organized so that I knew exactly what I was doing,
get it all organized, and then work solidly, well
maybe do six hours' revision without stopping and
that was the only way I could do it.

Woman: Yes, yes, and would you say to yourself, you know,   Q4
er, 'well, I'm going to do six hours today and I'm not
going to, go, I'm not going to have any fun until I've
done six hours'?

Man: Yeah, it was very much like that, er, an unpleasant
thing that you had to regulate. (*Mmm*)

Woman: I mean, well, I just hate revising anyway, I mean, you
know I hate that sort of thing, I mean, and in fact, I
did very little solid, sensible work, and, er what I'd
do is, because I was doing literature, I used to
re-read the novels, you know, on the course, and I'd
have er classical music on the radio, because, well, I ⎤ Q3
used to find that I got very bored if there was just
nothing, you know nothing at all in the background.

Man: Yes, I think of the people who do revise, there are
two sorts, there are those who work almost by topic,
they select a topic, and plough through it regardless,
and then, there are, well there are those who set
themselves a time limit of an amount to be done
rather than working through a specific topic regardless of the limit of time as I say . . .

pause

tone

Now you will hear the piece again.

> **TONE** Rewind the cassette to zero to hear the passage a second time.

WHERE THE
CLUES ARE

↓

pause

That is the end of the first part of the test.

pause

Second Part
You will hear part of a radio programme in which listeners express their views. For questions 9 to 20 tick one box to show whether each statement is true or false.

pause

tone

> *TONE* Set the counter on your cassette player to zero now.

TELL ALL

Simon Peters:	Hello, and welcome to *Tell All*, the programme in which we read your letters in response to whatever's been on Radio Five in the last week. And what's in our mailbag today? Well, Tuesday's science programme on weather had large numbers of you writing in. Someone signing himself J. Jones from Birmingham writes . . .
Reader:	What an interesting programme your *Weather Tomorrow* turned out to be. I was surprised, however, to hear Professor Strong's theory that we are going towards another Ice Age. I had always been taught that the earth was travelling nearer the sun!
Simon Peters:	You may be right, Mr Jones. But I don't suppose any of us'll be here when it happens. Mrs Marsh of Exeter is more concerned about immediate weather problems . . .
Reader:	It's all very well for the so-called experts to tell us what the weather's going to be like in the year 2084 – but that's no help to me today. Surely scientific research (and public money) would be better spent in making short-term weather forecasts more accurate?
Simon Peters:	A lot of listeners expressed the same point of

Q9

Q10

Q11

Q12

<table>
<tr><td></td><td>view. But Pat MacIntyre, who comes from Aberdeen in Scotland, raises yet another objection to the *Weather Tomorrow* team.</td><td>WHERE THE CLUES ARE
↓</td></tr>
</table>

Reader: So! They're experimenting to change our weather in Britain now, are they? But who wants less rain and more sun all the year round? No one I know would welcome a set pattern of weather, with every day the same, as they have in some countries. Granted, it might benefit our farmers. But what on earth would we talk about if we didn't have the changeable weather to discuss?

Q13

Simon Peters: I daresay we'd find something else. Food, for example, seems a subject close to your hearts, judging from the number of letters we've received on it. This week's no exception.

Q14

Reader: Dear Simon Peters, I'd like to protest about Radio Five's cookery series *Men in the Kitchen* on Wednesday afternoons . . .

Q15

Simon Peters: . . . writes Harry Priest from Cambridge.

Reader: The average male listener is quite capable of boiling an egg, so please don't waste programme time teaching us what we already know.

Simon Peters: Harry Priest wants more difficult recipes. Well, we have the producer and presenter of *Men in the Kitchen* here in the studio to er, reply to Mr Priest. David Battenburg. Dave – how about less *easy* cookery on your . . .

David Battenburg: I take Mr Priest's point, Simon. We've been doing basic stuff so far, um, to help beginners have a go, er, get some confidence. But we'll be going on to complete meals, etcetera in the next ten weeks, the sort of thing Mr Priest'll find more challenging, I hope.

Q16

Q17

Simon Peters: Let's hope so, too! And now finally in today's *Tell All* a couple of letters stimulated by the news that lending libraries may no longer be free to the public. This is what Fatima – no surname supplied I'm afraid – who lives at 16 Clifton Crescent in South West London – has to say about it.

Q19 - - - ￢

Q18

Reader: Students like myself cannot afford to buy all the books we study, and it will be very expensive for us when the libraries make us pay 20 pence for every book we borrow.

Simon Peters:	Cheer up, Fatima! It's only a suggestion, not a definite policy for libraries to charge. The last word comes from one of our Senior Citizens . . .
Reader:	What a good idea if libraries do charge 20 pence a book. We have to pay for spectacles, false teeth, and prescribed medicines – none of which we enjoy. So we should not expect our pleasures free. After all, people pay much more for an evening at the cinema or pub! Yours sincerely, Amy Wright (79 years).
Simon Peters:	Well, there's some more food for thought. And if there's anything you'd like to say – whether on something from this programme or, er, anything else you've heard on Radio Five that deserves some comment – then send your letter to me, Simon Peters, *Tell All*, Radio Five.

Q19

Q20

pause

tone

Now you will hear the piece again.

> ⋆⋆TONE⋆⋆ Rewind the cassette to zero to hear the passage a second time.

pause

That is the end of the second part of the test.

pause

Third Part
You will hear a recorded telephone announcement giving details about a cinema programme. For questions 21 to 25, fill in the gaps on the programme with the missing information.

pause

tone

> ⋆TONE⋆ Set the counter on your cassette player to zero now.

CINEMA ANNOUNCEMENT

This is the ABC Whiteladies cinema with recorded programme details. There are no booking facilities at this cinema.
In ABC 1 we retain *The Captain's Lady* (15 Certificate). Separate

Q21

programmes, doors open weekdays 1.00, 4.05 and 7.10, Sundays 3.30 and 6.40.

In ABC 2 we retain *Starfighters* (U Certificate). Separate programmes, doors open weekdays 1.10, 4.20 and 7.40, Sundays 3.30 and 6.30.

In ABC 3 we have *First Love* (15 Certificate). Separate programmes, doors open weekdays 2.15, 4.45 and 7.30, Sundays 4.20 and 7.10.

Q23
Q24

The late show for Friday is *The Captain's Lady*. Doors open 10.45 p.m.

Q25

Prices: adults £2.10 pence, children under 16 (*Starfighters* only) £1.10; over sixties, weekdays before six and Saturdays before four, £1.00.

Q22

If you require any further information please ring Bristol 730639. Thank you for calling.

pause

tone

Now you will hear the piece again.

⋆⋆TONE⋆⋆ Rewind the cassette to zero to hear the passage a second time.

---

pause

That is the end of the third part of the test.

pause

Fourth Part

You will hear a radio announcement telling the listeners about what programmes will be on during the day. For questions 26 to 30, tick one box to show whether each statement is true or false.

pause

tone

⋆TONE⋆ Set the counter on your cassette player to zero now.

RADIO ANNOUNCEMENT

Announcer: That was the fourth and final instalment of *Mission into Danger* by Ivor Wilkins. The programme was produced by Mary Hart. It will be repeated on Radio Four next Friday morning at 11 o'clock.

Q26

We have a little time before our next pro- WHERE THE
gramme, so let me tell you about some of your CLUES ARE
programmes on all our networks for the rest of ↓
the evening.

Here on Radio Four in just a minute, at 8.30, we
go over to Helston in Cornwall for this week's Q27
edition of our regular discussion programme *It's
My Opinion*, where the team will answer questions from an audience in the town hall.

Over on Radio Three, also at 8.30, we have a
concert of eighteenth-century Italian songs given
by Gwen Harding with the Helston Festival
Orchestra conducted by Frederick Davis.

If you're a sports enthusiast, there's a football
commentary on Radio Two at 9 o'clock. There's Q28
commentary on the whole of the second half of
the Scotland versus Brazil match from Rio de
Janeiro.

Moving on to later in the evening, after the 10
o'clock news, at 10.30 here on Radio Four we
have an investigation into credit card swindles Q29
called *Would you credit it?* In this programme Jack
Green asks what would or could happen if you
lost your credit card.

Just a word about Radio One, where this year's
London Pop Spectacular is being broadcast all Q30
evening until 11.30 live from the Royal Victoria
Hall in London.

Now it's 8.30, and we go over to Helston for
this week's edition of *It's My Opinion*.

pause

tone Now you will hear the piece again.

> ★★TONE★★ Rewind the cassette to zero to hear the passage a
> second time.

pause

That is the end of the fourth part of this test.

There will now be a pause to allow you to check your work. The
question papers will then be collected by your supervisor.

pause

tone

That is the end of the test.

Key to Practice Test 2

PAPER 1 READING COMPREHENSION

SECTION A

(See Study Notes p. 8 for Suggested method of working.)

1 A *practising*
   Meaning: In order to learn a skill you must actually use it regularly, not just study books about it.
   Distractor check:
   B *training*   You will have to prepare for the race by training for several weeks.
   C *exercising*   I know I should exercise more if I want to lose weight, but it's hard to find time.
   D *doing*   She'll be here in a moment, she's just doing her keep-fit exercises.

2 A *clever*
   Meaning: They think they sound more intelligent.
   Distractor check:
   B *intentional*   I do apologise, my rudeness was not at all intentional.
   C *skilled*   The doors can only be repaired by a really skilled craftsman.
   D *sensitive*   Be careful what you say, he's very sensitive about his work.

3 C *resign†*
   Meaning: He decided to give up his position and responsibilities on the committee.
   Distractor check:
   A *cancel*   I'm too upset to see anyone, please cancel all my appointments for today.
   B *postpone*   We must postpone our discussion until the manager arrives.
   D *prevent*   I shall take action to prevent such a situation from arising in the future.

4 C *source*
   Meaning: They went right up to the place where the river started.
   Distractor check:
   A *cause*   Do you know the cause of your illness?

† This is correct because it fits the structure of the sentence as well as the meaning.

B   *well*   The digging of a well made life much easier for the villagers.
D   *outlet*   Dirty water reaches the river from a factory outlet.

5   C   *label*
Meaning: He used a small piece of paper or plastic.
Distractor check:
A   *badge*   Before making the arrest, the detective showed his official badge.
B   *mark*   Each day, the prisoner made a mark on the wall with a knife so as to know how long he had been there.
D   *notice*   He pinned a notice on the school board giving details of the bike he wanted to sell.

6   C   *helping*
Meaning: He ate two portions of pudding.
Distractor check:
A   *load*   The lorry overturned and its load of vegetables fell into the road.
B   *pile*   The cat jumped onto the table and knocked over a pile of books.
D   *sharing*   I don't want to stay here if it means sharing a room with my brother!

7   A   *ability*†
Meaning: They knew he was good at his work.
Distractor check:
B   *possibility*   There's a possibility that I may be promoted quite soon.
C   *future*   My whole future will be decided by this interview.
D   *opportunity*   This trip to Paris is my only opportunity to work abroad this year.

8   A   *exchange*†
Meaning: I want to change some currency.
Distractor check:
B   *turn*   In the past, many chemists tried to turn lead into gold.
C   *alter*   You must not alter anything on the document after signing it.
D   *arrange*   The bank will arrange for money to be sent to you each week.

9   C   *relief*†
Meaning: We didn't have to worry about Geoffrey any more, which made us much happier.
Distractor check:
A   *anxiety*   His lateness caused us great anxiety.
B   *eyes*   In his father's eyes he can do no wrong.
D   *judgement*   I can give you the facts but you will have to make your own judgement.

† This is correct because it fits the structure of the sentence as well as the meaning.

10   A   *practice*†
            Meaning: He stopped working as a doctor in order to be a writer.
            Distractor check:
      B   *treatment*   Much modern treatment involves the use of powerful
            drugs.
      C   *procedure*   Before beginning the operation, the doctor explained the
            procedure to the patient.
      D   *prescription*   Take this prescription to the chemist to have the
            medicine made up.

11   D   *scratch*†
            Meaning: He may hurt you with his claws.
            Distractor check:
      A   *kick*   The frightened horse kicked a boy standing behind him.
      B   *tear*   Be careful not to tear your sleeve on that nail.
      C   *scream*   Sometimes my rheumatism is so bad I could scream with the
            pain.

12   B   *brand*
            Meaning: The makers claim that their product is the best!
            Distractor check:
      A   *model*   I know his car is an old Ford, but I don't know which model.
      C   *mark*   We can't use that symbol, it's a registered trademark.*
      D   *manufacture*   The company is involved in the manufacture of engine
            parts.
            *'mark' has no meaning in business English; check your dictionary.

13   B   *connection*
            Meaning: He thought they were committed by different people.
            Distractor check:
      A   *joint*   Make sure the joint in the pipe is watertight before you turn on
            the tap.
      C   *communication*   There must be no communication between candidates
            during the examination.
      D   *join*   He's mended the door so well that you have to look very closely
            to see where the join is.

14   C   *reach*
            Meaning: Medicines should be kept where children cannot get hold of
            them.
            Distractor check:
      A   *hold*   He lost his hold of the rope and fell to the ground.
      B   *hand*   He was dismissed out of hand, with no chance to defend
            himself.

† This is correct because it fits the structure of the sentence as well as the meaning.

    D   *grasp*   On shaking hands, I discovered that the old lady had a surprisingly firm grasp.

15 A   *substance*
       Meaning: The jar contained something that looked like jam.
       Distractor check:
    B   *material*   The box broke because the material it was made of was not strong enough.
    C   *solid*   We freeze the juice because it is easier to transport as a solid than as a liquid.
    D   *powder*   You buy the paint as a powder and mix it with water.

16 C   *fluent*
       Meaning: She spoke English very well indeed.
       Distractor check:
    A   *definite*   She has very definite ideas about what she is going to do with her life.
    B   *liquid*   Do you use powder or liquid soap?
    D   *national*   Because there are so many regional differences, it is hard to decide on a national policy.

17 A   *persuade*†
       Meaning: He may not agree to go.
       Distractor check:
    B   *suggest*   We suggested going, but he didn't like the idea.
    C   *make*   We tried to make him go, but he didn't want to.
    D   *prevent*   He wanted to go, but we prevented him from going because it was too dangerous.

18 D   *ladder*
       Meaning: He used the ladder to get up the tree.
       Distractor check:
    A   *scale*   The government was surprised by the scale of protest.
    B   *staircase*   The fire started at the foot of the staircase and quickly spread up through the centre of the building.
    C   *grade*   I won't get to university if I don't get a really good grade for maths.

19 A   *power*†
       Meaning: The Socialists became the government of that country six years ago.
       Distractor check:
    B   *force*   There was a curfew in force which prevented us from going out in the evening.

† This is correct because it fits the structure of the sentence as well as the meaning.

C   *control*   The Socialists are in control of the country.
D   *command*   He seemed a very young officer to be in command of so
many men.

20   C   *feel*
Meaning: You look to me as if you might be going to be sick.
Distractor check:
A   *fall*   It's vital that the Vice President should be available if the
President should fall sick.
B   *faint*   It was the intense heat which made him faint.
D   *become*   If you eat all that fruit you will become ill.

21   C   *leaning†*
Meaning: He used the wall for support.
Distractor check:
A   *stopping*   The bus tours the city, stopping at various places of interest.
B   *staying*   I'll be in the States for three weeks, staying with cousins.
D   *supporting*   They dug for hours, supporting the roof of the tunnel with
pieces of wood as they went along.

22   B   *waste*
Meaning: Fruit and vegetables which are unsold have to be thrown
away.
Distractor check:
A   *rot*   When one grape goes bad, the rot spreads through the bunch very
quickly.
C   *ruin*   The collapse of one large company can bring ruin to many small
businesses.
D   *rest*   If I carry these two bags, can you bring the rest?

23   C   *remaining†*
Meaning: The children had the food which the guests had not eaten.
Distractor check:
A   *additional*   As extra guests arrived we sent for additional supplies of
food.
B   *leaving*   We gave the headteacher a watch as a leaving present.
D   *left*   The children were allowed to eat the food that was left.

24   A   *pay†*
Meaning: She wanted to give them some money but she didn't have
any!
Distractor check:
B   *pay out*   We have to pay out a great deal of money to maintain the car.
C   *pay for*   I wouldn't dream of allowing you to pay for my ticket.

† This is correct because it fits the structure of the sentence as well as the meaning.

D *pay up* He'd been avoiding me for weeks, but he agreed to pay up when I went round to his house.

25 C *deputy*
   Meaning: The work was done by the junior manager.
   Distractor check:
   A *caretaker* The old caretaker was the only person who knew how to service the central heating boiler.
   B *officer* There was a letter in the newspaper from a retired naval officer complaining about government policy.
   D *commander* The commander was responsible for the loss of his ship.

SECTION B

FIRST PASSAGE

26 B
   because
   It was during the two-week summer holiday. (paragraph 1, lines 5–6)
   Distractor check:
   A It *was* too hot, but that's not the reason.
   C There is no suggestion of this.
   D There is no evidence for this in the passage.

27 D
   because
   It was plain black, 'without a belt or any ornaments'. (paragraph 1, lines 11–13)
   Distractor check:
   A A lot of jewellery – just one cross?
   B It was tight.
   C A white ribbon, not a white collar.

28 C
   because
   She had to roll a little as she walked. (paragraph 1, lines 9–11)
   Distractor check:
   A It doesn't say her dress made it difficult for her to walk.
   B We're not told that the necklace was heavy.
   D Her shoes made a noise, that's all.

29 D
   because
   She was 'conscious of being watched'. (paragraph 2, line 2)
   Distractor check:

A   The text doesn't say she heard anything.
B   There is no evidence for this in the passage.
C   She hadn't forgotten it!

30   C
because
She'd seen him there several times. (paragraph 3, lines 3–6)
Distractor check:
A   She just wondered if he was a policeman.
B   It doesn't say she had seen him on a bus.
D   There is no suggestion of this.

SECOND PASSAGE

31   C
because
Their ancient home was the forest. (paragraph 1, line 2)
Distractor check:
A   The other animals mentioned eat grass – pigs don't.
B   No, they were in the forest.
D   There is no evidence for this in the passage.

32   A
because
They found nuts, roots and dead animals there. (paragraph 1, lines 3, 5–6)
Distractor check:
B   They could have eaten waste food.
C   Nobody tried to develop improved breeds before that.
D   There is no suggestion of this.

33   C
because
Breeders were more interested in the larger animals. (paragraph 2, lines 2–3)
Distractor check:
A   Very fat pigs aren't mentioned.
B   They weren't replaced: different types were crossbred.
D   Not the important breeders.

34   B
because
They had flatter faces. (paragraph 2, line 9)
Distractor check:
A   They had shorter legs.
C   Shorter, not stronger.
D   Squarer, not rounder.

THIRD PASSAGE

35 B
    because
    They can see the sea from their bedroom balcony, and with at least seven
    floors and two restaurants it must be large. (Jean's card)
    Distractor check:
    A   With 'much hotter sunshine than in England'.
    C   It's not small and the beach is at least a short walk away.
    D   The historic town is 15 miles away.

36 D
    because
    They swim and sunbathe. (Helen's card)
    Distractor check:
    A   Only for Emma.
    B   There is no evidence for this in the passage.
    C   Only for Emma.

37 B
    because
    She prefers to be on the beach and this is what they've done most often.
    (Helen and Emma's cards)
    Distractor check:
    A   She seems to get pushed into things by one of the others.
    C   She only got her own way once.
    D   One of them seems to dominate.

38 B
    because
    This is what she describes most enthusiastically.
    Distractor check:
    A   That's what Jean likes.
    C   It's Jean that likes doing that.
    D   That's Emma's main interest.

39 A
    because
    She calls it 'superb'.
    Distractor check:
    B   She doesn't express an opinion.
    C   She doesn't like the hotel.
    D   One likes it more than the other two.

40 C
    because
    'I'm getting bored', she says.

Distractor check:
A   It's the bar that's too crowded.
B   She doesn't say so.
D   She doesn't say so.

PAPER 2   COMPOSITION

NOTES

(These notes may be consulted at various stages in your work – see Study Notes p. 11.)

1

Task Check
Remember – you're applying for a job
         – it's only for the summer
         – it's in your town

Register Check
Formal

Technique
If you haven't written this sort of letter for a while, check in a reference book the rules for setting out formal letters.

DANGER! Don't describe your town or the job: it's you they need to find out about.

Sample Plan

para 1 – have seen ad in newspaper, think self suitable

para 2 – knowledge of town (school project on local architecture)

       – like meeting all sorts of people

       – good general health

para 3 – special qualifications – 2 languages

para 4 – hope to be considered, etc.

2

Task Check
Story must be suitable for *young* children
Doesn't really matter if you knew it as a child, but better not to make it too up-to-date

Register Check
Informal speech

Technique
Write as you would speak to children, using everyday words and phrasal verbs. Check the note on varying your style under Practice Test 1, Composition 3, on p. 103.

DANGER! Avoid starting a traditional folk story which depends on special words which you only know in your own language. Don't choose a very long story or one with lots of repetition – it might be impossible to finish in time.

3

Look at the notes for Practice Test 1, Composition 3 on p. 103, then write a plan of your own for this title.

4

Task Check
You need to – give your opinion
– support your opinion with evidence

Register Check
Use fairly formal language, in keeping with the serious tone of the question.

Technique
A good way to give impact to this sort of composition is to begin with a description which illustrates what you are going to talk about, then to develop your argument from it, leading to your final conclusion.

Sample Plan

para 1 – description : teenager, all evening watching silly TV
programmes – no exercise, no homework, no communication
with family
para 2 – refer para 1, this is the bad side of TV, but what about old,
ill or lonely people ? Can be v. important
para 3 – good side of TV – educational programmes, current
affairs
para 4 – conclusion : many people watch too much TV, but if
we're discriminating, it can be useful

PAPER 3   USE OF ENGLISH

Question 1

1	food/rations/supplies/provisions	11	whether/if
2	ahead	12	there
3	them/quickly	13	after/by
4	set	14	given
5	rest/sleep	15	of
6	knew/guessed/realized	16	woke
7	previous	17	few/dozen
8	left/placed	18	but/except
9	were	19	tied/wrapped/fastened
10	in	20	bag/basket

Common error check

4 went ✗
    'went off' means 'went away', but who did they go away *from*? They merely
    started their day's journey, which is what 'set off' means.

9 did ✗
    'they' means the gifts! Look at 'touched' – if 'they' meant the men, the verb
    would be 'they did not touch'.

11 that ✗
    Compare: I didn't know that Marcus was married (which means 'I assumed
    he was single', with: I didn't know whether Marcus was married (meaning
    'I thought he might be married, but I wasn't sure').

Question 2

a) If you │ *don't get* │ a visa you can't visit the United States.
         │ *do not get* │
         │ *haven't (got)* │
         │ *have not (got)* │

b) Peter asked if │ *he could borrow* │ *Janet's* │ typewriter.
                  │ *Janet could lend him* │ *her* │

c) She has │ *worked* as a secretary │ *for five years.*
   She's   │ *been working* as a secretary │ *since.........(year).*
           │ *been* a secretary │

d) I don't know │ *as much* │ about it │ *as* │ she does.
                │ *so much* │

e) My French friend isn't │ *used* │ *to driving* │ on the left.
                          │ *accustomed* │

f) The owner of the house │ *is thought* │ *to be* │ abroad.

g) If we │ *had had enough* │ money │ *we would have gone* │ on holiday.
         │   │   │ *we could have gone* │

h) The sea was too │ *rough for* │ *the* │ *children to go swimming.* │

i) I wish │ *you had passed* │ your driving test.
          │ *you had managed to pass* │
          │ *you had succeeded in passing* │
          │ *you hadn't failed* │

j) I │ *had* │ *my car serviced* │ last week.
     │ *got* │

Question 3
a) timetable/time-table/time table
b) in/on time
c) by the time
d) out of time
e) time to time

Question 4
a) tools
b) seasons
c) meals
d) furniture
e) vehicles

Question 5

a) I expect | you will be | surprised | to get | a | letter |
you'll be		when you get	this	
you must be				
you are				

   from | me.

b) As | you can see | from | the | address above | I am | in hospital.
   | | | | | I'm |

c) Last Wednesday | I had | an accident | when | I was driving | to work.

d) A | child | ran | out | in front of | my car and | I had | to stop |

   so suddenly that | the | car behind | crashed | into | me.

e) Luckily | I was wearing | my | seatbelt so | I was not |
   | | | | I have not been |

   injured badly although | I may have | to stay | here
I might have	
I shall have	
I'll have	

   | until next Friday.
   | till next Friday.

f) It is | very boring and | I would be pleased | to see you | if you have
   | | I'll be pleased | |
   | | I'd be pleased | |

   | any spare time.
   | a little spare time.
   | a bit of spare time.

g) Visiting hours | are | 7.00 to 9.00 | in the evening.
   | | | every evening.

h) I hope | you are able | to come.
   | you're able |
   | you will be able |
   | you'll be able |

Question 6

Step one

Identify the good and bad points.
These are marked with a tick (√) and a cross (✗) on the sample pages (pp. 134–5).

Step two

Make notes.

<u>Notes</u>

Best flat: N. st   2nd best : B.Ave

because √ close college   because   √ lovely area
       √ " shops   √ garden
       √ big lounge   √ central heating
       √ quite modern   √ large & clean (2 beds)

drawbacks: ✗ busy street   <u>but</u> : ✗ 4 miles fr. college
        ? share bedroom   ✗ 15 minutes bus stop
                          ? landlord

Bad flat – M. Hill
✗ everything !
except price

Note: As this is an *opinion*, you may have different ideas, but you must be able to give logical reasons for them using the information given.

Step three

Complete the letter.
(See the sample pages.)

SAMPLE PAGE (see p. 133)

6 *Susan Bates and Janet Peel are going to move to London to study at a college there.*
Susan has come to London before the term starts to look for a flat for them both.
She has visited four flats and is writing a letter to Janet to tell her about them.
Look at the notes Susan made about each flat and then complete her letter.

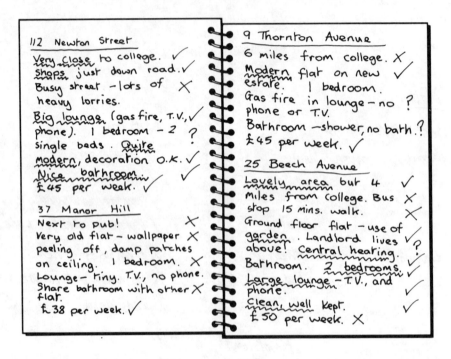

Dear Janet,

Just a quick letter to tell you what I've been doing. I went to see
four flats today and I liked one of them very much. It was in a road
called *Newton Street* and I think it would suit us very well because
it's very close to the college and also to the local shops. It's got
a big lounge with a gas fire, TV and a phone. It's quite modern and
the decoration isn't bad. The bathroom's really nice, and
best of all, we can afford it, as it's £45 a week!

SAMPLE PAGE

However it did have a couple of drawbacks. *Unfortunately it's on a busy street and there's a lot of noise from heavy lorries. However, that shouldn't be so bad when we're in, at weekends. Also we'll have to share the bedroom, I hope you don't mind.*

There was another flat in *Beech Avenue* which was nearly as good. *It's in a lovely area and has a garden. It's large and clean and has central heating. There are two bedrooms as well, which would be very nice, and it's well-equipped.*

I don't think it would be as suitable for us as the other one because *it's so far from the college, about 4 miles in fact. And it's 15 minutes from the bus stop. Also the landlord lives upstairs, which might not be very pleasant.*

One of the flats I saw was really dreadful. I'm amazed the landlord wanted so much for it. I doubt if you'd even consider living there because *it's old, damp, small, badly-equipped and worst of all, next to a pub! Imagine the noise when we're trying to study in the evenings.*

I'd better finish so that I can post this. Ring me as soon as you can and let me know what you think so I can make all the arrangements.

Yours,

Susan

PAPER 4   LISTENING COMPREHENSION

FIRST PART

Channel swimming
1 hat/cap
2 high tide
3 12/twelve
4 30/thirty

5 grease
6 allowed
7 being disqualified

SECOND PART

Customer complaint
 8 C
 9 D
10 D

11 D
12 A

THIRD PART

Driving lesson
13 r
14 q

15 p
16 s

FOURTH PART

Stratford Leisureline information
17 204016
18 30/thirty minutes/half an hour
19 High Street
20 Motor (car)
21 294466

22 toy trains
23 3.30/half past three
24 Hall
25 11 a.m./eleven o'clock
26 Sunday(s)

TAPESCRIPT

> The rubric on this cassette follows exactly the wording of the
> Cambridge First Certificate Exam. To save space on the cassette
> the repeats have not been included. At the beginning of each
> passage, set the counter on your cassette player to zero. At the
> end of the passage, rewind the cassette to zero to hear the
> passage again. **Remember, you should hear each passage twice
> only!**

Cambridge First Certificate Listening Test

TEST NUMBER 2

You will be given a question paper for First Certificate Test 2.
Your supervisor will give you further instructions. On the
question paper you will see spaces for your name and index
number, and questions for each part of the test. Each part of the
test will be heard twice. There will be pauses to allow you to
look through the questions before each part, and other pauses
to let you think about your answers. At the end of every pause
you will hear this sound.

tone

The tape will now be stopped while question papers are given
out. You must ask any questions now, as you will not be
allowed to speak during the test.

pause

First Part
You will hear a radio interview about swimming the English
Channel. For questions 1 to 7, fill in the gaps on the information
sheet.

pause

tone

> ★TONE★ Set the counter on your cassette player to zero now.

CHANNEL SWIMMING

		WHERE THE CLUES ARE

Interviewer:	So you in fact supervise all Channel swims?	↓
Ken Richards:	Yes, everybody who wishes to have their swim officially recorded must come to us first, and then we put our official observer on the pilot boat. They have very clear instructions as to what must be done, no artificial aids whatso-	
	ever. We tell them that they can wear a cap, a	Q1
	bathing costume and lanolin grease, and that's	Q5 - - - - -
	all. They walk in at this side, get out at the other side clear of the water and then they've swum the Channel.	
Interviewer:	Rather them than me! Now just tell us what happens. They start here. What is the best time, first of all, of the year, and what is the best time of the day to do it?	
Ken Richards:	Well, it must be warm, Janet, so July, August, September are the best months and then we give the swimmers a table of the tides which shows them high tides at Dover.	
Interviewer:	Do they start on high tide?	
Ken Richards:	They start an hour and a half after high tide.	Q2
Interviewer:	And what sort of style do they use? Is it always the crawl, or . . .	
Ken Richards:	It is the crawl, if you're going to make a fast pace; there are swimmers who've done it breast stroke, of course, and that obviously is very much slower.	
Interviewer:	What about training, how long do you have to train before you can even attempt it?	
Ken Richards:	Well, at least twelve months. To start with, you	Q3
	want two hours in the morning, two hours in the evening. You want several six hour swims and then several ten hour swims before you	
	can hope to tackle the Channel. We recommend	Q4
	at least thirty hours' swimming each week in your last three weeks.	
Interviewer:	Yes, erm, well an obvious question, the cold.	Q5 - - - - -
	Does grease really keep out the cold?	
Ken Richards:	Ah, well, I think it's more psychological than real, Janet. It probably eases the shock when they first get in the water, but . . .	
Interviewer:	And what about feeding – they're allowed to be	Q6
	fed from the boat, is that right?	
Ken Richards:	Oh yes, yes, they can't hang on to anything, of course. They'd be immediately disqualified if	Q7

138

they even hung onto the boat for one second, unless of course the boat hit them, (*laughs*) but they are handed drinks, er, usually on the end of a sort of er, well, a fishing rod, with a wire ring on the end in which you put a plastic cup, or you can hand it straight down to them if they can get close enough to the boat.

Interviewer: Do they swim the whole time or do they sort of lie on their back and rest?

Ken Richards: Well, they're allowed to, of course, but they don't. They just keep at it, remember that they're all well trained, they've been doing it for a very long time.

pause

tone

Now you will hear the piece again.

★★TONE★★ Rewind the cassette to zero to hear the passage a second time.

---

pause

That is the end of the first part of the test.

pause

Second Part

You will hear a conversation in a shop between a customer and two people who work there. For questions 8 to 12 tick one of the boxes A, B, C or D to show the correct answer.

pause

tone

★TONE★ Set the counter on your cassette player to zero now.

CUSTOMER COMPLAINT

Customer: Er, excuse me . . .

Assistant 1: Sorry, I'll be with you in a moment. (*Oh*) I'm with another customer.

Customer: But I was before that customer.

Assistant 1: Sorry, but I am busy at the moment. Excuse me.

	I'll get somebody else to serve you. Mr Harding, could you serve this customer, please? I'm dealing with somebody else, and this customer has been waiting some time.	Q8
Assistant 2:	All right. Yes, sir. Can I help you?	
Customer:	Well, I hope so. I bought this cassette here the other day, and I'm afraid it's faulty.	
Assistant 2:	Er . . . Got your receipt, have you?	
Customer:	Well, no, I haven't actually.	
Assistant 2:	Well, we can't do anything without a receipt, I'm afraid.	
Customer:	Oh, yes you can. I know my rights. I don't have to have any receipt to change faulty goods.	
Assistant 2:	OK. What seems to be the matter with it?	
Customer:	Well, it keeps getting stuck in my cassette player.	Q9
Assistant 2:	Getting stuck? It's probably your machine. Here, let me have a look at the cassette.	
Customer:	Here you are. It isn't my machine. I'm sure of that because . . .	
Assistant 2:	Oh well, the cassette looks perfectly all right to me. I can't see anything wrong with it. We've sold hundreds of these and you're the first person to bring one back with a complaint. Must be your machine.	Q10
Customer:	Well, look, how can it be my machine?	
Assistant 2:	Well, you know, it probably needs servicing.	
Customer:	No. No. What I mean is, I've got over a hundred cassettes, and the one you're holding is the only one that sticks, and what's more . . .	
Assistant 2:	Well, that may be, but I still can't see anything wrong. How long have you had this cassette, sir?	Q11
Customer:	I was going to say, I was going to say I tried it in my brother's machine and it stuck there. Now that would seem to prove that it is not my machine.	
Assistant 2:	Well, have you been winding it back properly, sir?	
Customer:	Well, I think so – the way I always do.	
Assistant 2:	You've done it by hand or you did it in the machine? (*Machine*) You haven't been sticking a pencil in there by any chance?	
Customer:	Certainly not! Certainly not! Now look, why don't you give me a replacement and I'll be quite happy. One the same, that's all I want . . .	
Assistant 2:	I'm sorry, sir, without a receipt it's, it's absolutely impossible. I've got absolutely no proof that you	

140

	bought it here.	WHERE THE CLUES ARE

Customer: But I *did* buy it here a few days ago.

Assistant 2:   I see . . . (*sigh*)

Customer: Look – can I see the manager, please?

Assistant 2:   You can certainly see the manager.

Customer: Perhaps he'll sort it out?

Assistant 2:   I'm afraid he's, I'm afraid the manager's at lunch,   Q12
sir. You'll have to deal with me.

Customer: At lunch? What time does he come back?

Assistant 2:   Well, he won't be back today – he's, er, got half a
day off, sir.

Customer: Look, it was a young girl that served me last time.
Perhaps she will recognize me. It was only a few
days ago.

Assistant 2:   Ah, a young girl, was she a fair-haired girl, sir?

Customer: Yes, (*Yes, I see*), she was rather, rather nice looking . . .

Assistant 2:   She no longer works here, sir.

Customer: Oh, I see . . .

Assistant 2:   Mm . . .

Customer: Well, I shall just have to come back later and see
the manager.

Assistant 2:   I should do that, sir (*Yes, mm, right*) Come back
tomorrow morning.

Customer: Tomorrow morning? Yes, right.

pause

tone

Now you will hear the piece again.

> ★★TONE★★ Rewind the cassette to zero to hear the passage a
> second time.

pause

That is the end of the second part of the test.

pause

Third Part
You will hear a driving instructor teaching a man how to drive.
For numbers 13 to 16 fill in the boxes with the letter for each
difficulty that the driver meets in the order in which they
happen.

pause

tone

WHERE THE
CLUES ARE

↓

★TONE★ Set the counter on your cassette player to zero now.

DRIVING LESSON

Instructor: Right, go on then; this time keep your foot down on the accelerator a bit more. Oh gosh, no, not as much as that; no no . . .

Learner: I'm sorry I can't seem to push, either my foot goes right down and I make this awful noise. Oh, all right I'll try again.

Instructor: OK. Well, let's just try again then. Now, ah, that's much better, right off we go then, check your mirror.

Learner: Into first gear, check my mirror, there's nothing at the back . . .

Instructor: Right, now indicate.

Learner: Yes . . . Right, should I pull out now?

Instructor: Into first (*Yes*) right now off we go.

Learner: What about this cyclist that's coming up on the other side?

Instructor: No, just keep going steadily, he's all right he can see you. OK that's it, fine, all right steadily on down the road. Now change up into second, now.

Learner: OK.

Instructor: That's it.

Learner: Do I stay in second?

Instructor: Yes, just stay in second.

Learner: I'm not going very fast.

Instructor: Well no, but, er, let's just take it easy for a little bit. Now see that pedestrian crossing ahead?   Q14

Learner: Yes.

Instructor: That's it, now right . . .

Learner: Shall I stop? There's nobody there.

Instructor: No, there's nobody there so off we go, that's it, just keep going steadily, now you must keep a watch out for pedestrians who are crossing the road who are not on crossings and there are plenty of those.

Learner: But I have right of way, don't I? I don't have to pull up for them?

Instructor: Well, it pays to be very careful, because once you've knocked somebody down it's too late. You see that old lady there?   Q15

Learner: Yes.

142

Instructor:	Now she's dithering on the edge, er, . . . and that's WHERE THE
	it, she's not going to cross the road. CLUES ARE
Learner:	Shall I stop?
Instructor:	No, keep going . . .
Learner:	I think I'd rather let her across . . .
Instructor:	No, you just keep going.
Learner:	I don't feel very happy. Oh, OK.
Instructor:	Keep going, that's it, that's right; turn, turn left at the next corner, so what are you going to do?
Learner:	Shall I stop?
Instructor:	Indicate. No! No, indicate now.
Learner:	So I indicate; (*Check your mirror*) now do I have to stop before, before I go round, what about that van coming out, he's got his emergency flashers winking, should I let him come first?
Instructor:	No, he's stopped so we'll have to go slowly round him but keep going, he's stopped . . .
Learner:	I don't think I can get the car through there, can I?
Instructor	Oh, yes, yes.
Learner:	Shall I let him, indicate for him to come?
Instructor:	No, let him go, he's stopped he'll be all right, you keep going around the corner. Ah, that's it, now off we go, this is a little quieter side street.

CLUES ARE ↓

Q16

pause

tone

Now you will hear the piece again.

★★TONE★★ Rewind the cassette to zero to hear the passage a second time.

---

pause

That is the end of the third part of the test.

pause

Fourth Part
You will hear a recorded telephone announcement for tourists.
For questions 17 to 26 fill in the missing information in the
spaces provided.

pause

tone

WHERE THE
CLUES ARE

★TONE★ Set the counter on your cassette player to zero now.

STRATFORD LEISURELINE

Welcome to Stratford-upon-Avon Leisureline Service for visitors and residents. I will first give details of the places of historical interest, followed by entertainments and events during the coming months.

The places of interest to see are: Shakespeare's Birthplace and Centre in Henley Street; Anne Hathaway's cottage, the home of Shakespeare's wife, in Shottery village; New Place, the site of Shakespeare's retirement home; Hall's Croft, where his daughter and son-in-law lived; and Mary Arden's house, his mother's home, situated at Wilmcote. Details of opening times and admission charges are obtainable from Stratford-upon-Avon 204016. — Q17

Visit the medieval parish church, Holy Trinity, where Shakespeare and his family are buried. In Waterside you will find the World of Shakespeare Theatre, giving a half-hour audio-visual — Q18
show of Elizabethan life. And the Shakespearian theme is continued at Louis Tussaud's waxworks in Henley Street. There is also Harvard House in High Street, the home of Catherine — Q19
Rogers, the mother of the founder of Harvard University, USA. And in Shakespeare Street you can visit the motor museum. A — Q20
brass-rubbing centre is in the Royal Theatre Summerhouse, adjacent to the theatre. Other places within easy reach are: Charlecote House, Ragley Hall, Coughton Court, Warwick Castle and Kenilworth Castle. Many guided tours to these and other places are operated by Guide Friday Ltd, Henley Street. Ring Stratford-upon-Avon 294466. — Q21

Forthcoming entertainments and events of interest for the month of January are as follows: The Royal Shakespeare Theatre plays in current performance are: *Macbeth, Much Ado, King Lear, The Tempest* and *The Taming of the Shrew*. For booking information, please ring the booking office, Stratford-upon-Avon 295623. On 1st January, there's a sale of old toy trains at the — Q22
Parish Church Hall from 10.30 a.m. to 3.30 p.m. On the 6th, 7th — Q23
and 8th of January, Shottery Youth Theatre present *The Land of Make-Believe* at the Shottery Memorial Hall. We hope you enjoy — Q24
your visit to Stratford-upon-Avon, truly in the heart of England. For more information, ring the Tourist Information Centre on Stratford-upon-Avon 293127, winter office hours 11.00 a.m. to — Q25
5.00 p.m., Monday to Saturday. Thank you for calling. — Q26

pause

tone

Now you will hear the piece again.

⋆⋆TONE⋆⋆ Rewind the cassette to zero to hear the passage a
second time.

---

pause

That is the end of the fourth part of this test.

There will now be a pause to allow you to check your work. The
question papers will then be collected by your supervisor.

pause

tone

That is the end of the test.

Key to Practice Test 3

PAPER 1 READING COMPREHENSION

SECTION A

(See Study Notes p. 8 for Suggested method of working.)

1 A *fade*
      Meaning: They began to lose their colour.
      Distractor check:
   B *die* The flowers began to die because they weren't getting enough water.
   C *dissolve* Sugar will dissolve in hot water.
   D *melt* Be careful, the chocolate will melt in the sun.

2 C *distinguish†*
      Meaning: They cannot tell the difference, for example, between 'fan' and 'fun'.
      Distractor check:
   A *separate* Although he was frightened, he managed to separate the men who were fighting.
   B *differ* The accents of foreigners who are learning English differ widely.
   D *solve* I couldn't solve the crossword puzzle: it was too difficult.

3 A *rattled*
      Meaning: The windows repeatedly made a noise hitting against the wooden frames.
      Distractor check:
   B *slapped* When he insulted her, she slapped his face.
   C *flapped* The sheets hanging on the clothes line flapped in the wind.
   D *shocked* I was shocked to hear such terrible news.

4 A *accustomed†*
      Meaning: I hardly notice it any more; I'm used to it.
      Distractor check:
   B *familiar* I'm quite familiar with London – I've visited it often so I've got to know it well.

† This is correct because it fits the structure of the sentence as well as the meaning.

C *unconscious* He smiled happily, unconscious of the embarrassment he was causing.

D *aware* The baby's gradually becoming aware of its environment.

5 B *made†*
Meaning: He forced her to do it.
Distractor check:

A *let* He didn't let her have a day off.

C *insisted* He insisted that she trained every day.
or He insisted on her training every day.

D *caused* His attitude caused a lot of bad feeling between them.

6 A *invent††*
Meaning: She made up a story.
Distractor check:

B *combine* How do you combine a full-time job with bringing up two children?

C *manage* Did she manage to convince them that she was telling the truth?

D *lie* She had to lie (*or* 'tell a lie').

7 D *flat*
Meaning: We had a puncture.
Distractor check:

A *broken* The jack was broken, so we couldn't lift the tyre off the ground.

B *cracked* The wing mirror was cracked, but we could still use it.

C *bent* The key was bent, so it wouldn't go in the lock.

8 D *down*
Meaning: They rejected her application.
Distractor check:

A *back* The police were turning cars back at the road block.

B *up* This old photograph album turned up when I was clearing the attic.

C *over* When they had caught the escaped prisoner, they turned him over to the police.

9 D *common†*
Meaning: They both prefer sandy soil.
Distractor check:

A *similar* The two flowers look very similar.

B *same* All these flowers come from the same garden.

† This is correct because it fits the structure of the sentence as well as the meaning.

     C   *shared*   The only feature shared by these two flowers is their strong scent.

10   A   *intervals*
           Meaning: There were two breaks during the performance.
           Distractor check:
     B   *rests*   She only sleeps four hours a night, but she has frequent rests during the day.
     C   *interruptions*   We couldn't have a proper meeting because there were so many interruptions.
     D   *gaps*   I have a very busy schedule tomorrow but I think there's a gap in the afternoon when I could see you.

11   C   *pulled down*
           Meaning: They're going to be demolished.
           Distractor check:
     A   *laid out*   Her conclusions are laid out clearly in the report.
     B   *run down*   He was run down by a drunken driver.
     D   *knocked out*   England was knocked out of the World Cup by Argentina.

12   D   *appointment*
           Meaning: The appointment was for nine in the morning.
           Distractor check:
     A   *order*   I've placed an order for the new book at my booksellers.
     B   *date*   He has a date with his girlfriend tonight.
     C   *assignment*   The teacher gave the class a difficult assignment for homework.

13   D   *loads*
           Meaning: Fifteen tons is the maximum amount of goods that they may carry.
           Distractor check:
     A   *masses*   They have masses of rubbish in their garden.
           (Note: The word 'loads' can also be used informally in this way, meaning 'lots of'.)
     B   *sizes*   The shirts come in three different sizes: small, medium and large.
     C   *measures*   Mix one measure of flour with two measures of milk.

14   A   *undertook*†
           Meaning: He agreed to make the attempt, although it was dangerous.
           Distractor check:
     B   *agreed*   He agreed to go on the mission.

† This is correct because it fits the structure of the sentence as well as the meaning.

C   *promised*   He promised to go on the mission.
D   *entered*   He entered for the competition.

15   C   *check†*
Meaning: You must make sure that it is fastened.
Distractor check:
A   *examine*   The guard had to examine my passport carefully before letting me across the frontier.
B   *secure*   You should secure your bicycle to the fence with a padlock.
D   *guarantee*   We guarantee to replace this TV if it goes wrong within twelve months.

16   D   *caught*
Meaning: He became ill.
Distractor check:
A   *took*   He took some medicine for his illness.
B   *suffered*   He suffered from diabetes during the later years of his life.
C   *infected*   Millions of people around the world are infected with malaria.

17   C   *niece*
Meaning: The daughter of a sister or brother.
Distractor check:
A   *nephew*   The son of a sister or brother.
B   *cousin*   The child of an uncle or aunt.
D   *relation*   I've got lots of relations, but only one grandson.

18   B   *laughter*
Meaning: He obviously thought it was funny.
Distractor check:
A   *smiles*   Her nervousness soon disappeared when she saw the friendly smiles on their faces.
C   *amusement*   Much to the amusement of the audience, the speaker dropped his notes.
D   *enjoyment*   His novels have provided enjoyment for millions of readers.

19   B   *turned†*
Meaning: The lights changed to green.
Distractor check:
A   *exchanged*   Before returning to England, I exchanged all my francs for pounds.
C   *removed*   They've removed the traffic lights and put a roundabout there instead.

† This is correct because it fits the structure of the sentence as well as the meaning.

D   *shone*   The moon shone brightly in the clear night sky.

20 C   *smartly*
       Meaning: You should wear good clothes and look tidy.
       Distractor check:
   A   *finely*   She was much too finely dressed to do any work.
   B   *boldly*   Although she was frightened, she spoke out boldly.
   D   *clearly*   My English isn't very good. Please speak very slowly and clearly.

21 D   *bargain*
       Meaning: Something that's cheap at the price.
       Distractor check:
   A   *trade*   Do you know anyone in the second-hand car trade?
   B   *shopping*   We went to the market to do some shopping.
   C   *chance*   There's a chance we'll find what we want.

22 D   *fit†*
       Meaning: He won't be in a suitable condition to play.
       Distractor check:
   A   *skilled*   He's a very skilled player.
   B   *capable*   He won't be capable of playing.
   C   *possible*   I don't think it'll be possible for him to play.

23 D   *suits*
       Meaning: The colour looks good on you.
       Distractor check:
   A   *fits*   This coat doesn't fit me – it's too tight.
   B   *matches*   He's wearing a blue tie which matches the colour of his eyes.
   C   *shows*   That style shows you to your best advantage.

24 A   *avoided*
       Meaning: Most accidents are due to carelessness.
       Distractor check:
   B   *excluded*   He was excluded from the team because he was too unfit.
   C   *protected*   My house is protected by a burglar alarm.
   D   *preserved*   Meat can be preserved by the addition of salt.

25 A   *break*
       Meaning: They find it difficult to stop.
       Distractor check:
   B   *beat*   In the football match today, Liverpool beat Chelsea 2–1.
   C   *breathe*   Smoking indoors makes the air unpleasant to breathe.
   D   *cough*   Smokers usually cough a lot.

† This is correct because it fits the structure of the sentence as well as the meaning.

SECTION B

FIRST PASSAGE

26   A
     because
     They have stopped hunting and collecting food. (paragraph 1, lines 2–4)
     Distractor check:
     B   There is no evidence of this in the passage.
     C   The text doesn't say they are the only non-human society like this.
     D   There are other non-human societies like this, too.

27   B
     because
     They are the gardeners and nurses. (paragraph 2, lines 1–3)
     Distractor check:
     A   This is done by the third group mentioned.
     C   This is the work of the largest ants of all.
     D   We don't know this. Other tasks sound more strenuous.

28   C
     because
     The scientist measured how much work they did and how much energy
     they used.
     Distractor check:
     A   There is no evidence of this in the passage.
     B   There is no suggestion of this.
     D   We don't learn about the ants' feelings!

29   B
     because
     He repeated the experiment for each group – it was a series of experiments.
     (paragraph 3, line 5)
     Distractor check:
     A   No, he worked at it systematically.
     C   The third paragraph mentions 'the nest'.
     D   Presumably the nest he was observing was disturbed when he made
         different ants try each other's jobs.

30   B
     because
     Each group of ants had a specific set of jobs. (paragraph 1, lines 7–8,
     paragraph 2)
     Distractor check:

A   Some of the ants were not ideally suited to their jobs, so presumably others would have done the work faster.
C   Look carefully at the second paragraph!
D   Apparently some of them are not ideally suited to what they do.

SECOND PASSAGE

31 A
because
Children compare their own performances with those of others and make any necessary changes. (paragraph 1, lines 2–4)
Distractor check:
B   The author says they should correct their own mistakes.
C   By observing skilled people, not listening to their explanations.
D   There is no suggestion of this.

32 B
because
He thinks they should let children find their own mistakes. (paragraph 1, lines 8–12)
Distractor check:
A   On the contrary, he says they should give the child the answer book.
C   This is what he says they should do, but they don't.
D   He says teachers don't encourage children to help each other.

33 D
because
They are things children learn without being taught. (paragraph 1, lines 4–8)
Distractor check:
A   There is no suggestion of this.
B   There is no suggestion of this, either.
C   There is no comparison made of children's and adults' skills.

34 B
because
Children should learn to measure their own knowledge and understanding. (paragraph 2, lines 1–2, 5–7)
Distractor check:
A   No, they have to learn to measure themselves, not the children's progress.
C   Not according to this author.
D   There is no suggestion of this.

35   C
   because
   Children learn to be too dependent on their teachers instead of making
   judgements for themselves. (Find all the sentences beginning 'Let . . .')
   A   He thinks they aren't independent enough.
   B   He thinks they don't learn to criticize themselves.
   D   He thinks they'll have basic skills, but not be able to make judgements.

THIRD PASSAGE

36   B
   because
   The hire charge doesn't cover personal accident insurance.
   Distractor check:
   A   That's what 'Full insurance cover' means.
   C   That's covered under (b) in the list.
   D   That's also covered under (b) in the list.

37   B
   because
   That is the minimum time for the low price rental.
   Distractor check:
   A   Three days is the minimum at the low price.
   C   You may not be able to hire a car at all if you leave it till you reach
        London!
   D   That's how you can be sure to get a car; it doesn't affect the cost.

38   D
   because
   It's included in the charge, so provided the driver keeps the receipt, the
   company will refund the cost.
   Distractor check:
   A   But the company will repay the cost.
   B   The driver pays and then gets a receipt in order to get the cost from the
        company.
   C   No, by the charge for hiring, which also includes insurance.

39   A
   because
   There is a variety of types of vehicle available in each price range.
   Distractor check:
   B   But the hire charges cover unlimited mileage.
   C   There is no suggestion of this.
   D   That's something the driver must pay for.

40   B
     because
     It's equivalent to the cancellation charge.
     Distractor check:
     A   The payment in full is returned, minus £12.
     C   The £12 is part of the hire cost.
     D   Six weeks is the time needed to guarantee a booking.

PAPER 2   COMPOSITION

NOTES

(These notes may be consulted at various stages in your work. See Study Notes p. 11.)

1

Task Check
You need to – give details of the recorder
            – say when and where it was bought
            – describe fault
            – ask for repair

Register Check
Formal, this is a business letter.

Technique
If you haven't written this sort of letter for a while, check in a reference book the rules for setting out business letters. How should you begin and end?

DANGER! This is not a letter of complaint. Don't be angry, just politely request the repair.

Sample Plan

para 1 – bought enclosed recorder Model RCR3, 2 weeks ago at London Sound Centre, Oxford St

para 2 – fine at first, now no sound when tape played (something loose inside?)

para 3 – please repair, soon?

para 4 – can be contacted mornings only, phone number, if problems
  – thank, yours, etc.

2

Task Check
You need to – welcome them and tell them about the town (it doesn't really have to be your local town).

Register Check
Friendly (but slightly formal as you're the mayor), remembering that it's speech, not writing, and your audience is not adult.

Technique
Keep in mind all the time the audience you are addressing.

Sample Plan

para 1 – welcome, pleased to see them, hope had good journey, not too tired

para 2 – places they'll visit: museum, wildlife sanctuary, castle

para 3 – activities: athletics meeting, mountain walk

para 4 – hope enjoy visit and more contacts in future

3

Task Check
You must – describe the journey (it needn't be a real one, but that is probably
            the easiest way)
          – describe a particularly unpleasant person, either a passenger or an
            official whom you meet during the journey (he or she can be
            invented, of course)

Register Check
Probably informal, but this is really up to you.

Technique
This will be a first person narrative. A good way would be to describe a journey
you know well and insert into it an incident in which someone unpleasant
spoils the journey for you. Vary the pace by using direct speech for the central
incident – but not too much!

DANGER! Don't let either the journey or the person dominate too much. Keep a
balance.

Sample Plan

para 1 – leaving college, tired, settle in train, crowded but
          get seat, thinking about getting home
para 2 – young man, last seat in compartment, rude
          manner, smoking, noisy music, insulting people
          (contrast his speech style / polite requests others)
para 3 – relief when he leaves, extra happy to get home

4

Task Check
You need to – define what you understand by 'much stricter punishments'
            – explain what effect you think they would have

Register Check
Use fairly formal language, in keeping with the serious tone of the question.

DANGER! Don't turn your composition into an emotional argument about
capital or corporal punishment, this would be too narrow.

Sample Plan

para 1 — compare two punishments for vandalism (breaking a door) a) mending it & b) 1 month in prison

para 2 — vandal's feelings a) perhaps thinks he got off lightly, b) angry and shocked. BUT a) has faced results of his action

para 3 — important questions: which is most likely to re-offend? Which punishment was most useful to victim?

para 4 — my opinion: stricter punishments only help if they are appropriate, giving criminal sense of responsibility

---

PAPER 3   USE OF ENGLISH

Question 1

1 number/group
2 by/near/at/beside
3 them/that/it
4 rose/towered/appeared
5 what
6 see/watch
7 over/across
8 this/that/the
9 with
10 a

11 could
12 coloured/patterned
13 as
14 other/distant/opposite/far
15 its/their
16 crowd/number/group
17 from
18 Suddenly
19 causing
20 each/the

Common error check:

5 that ✗
Check your relative pronouns!

13 when ✗
This would mean they couldn't see the bundles all the time, but the crowd of people are moving together in one direction, so we know they can.

16   line ✕

This is too disciplined. A line could march straight through the crowd, not have to work its way, which implies 'with some difficulty'. Also, soldiers are unlikely to be in a line if they're off duty, which seems to be the case here.

Question 2

a) Travelling │ *by air always makes me* │ nervous.

b) The car │ *was too expensive* │ *for him.* │
   │ *cost more than he could afford.*
   │ *was so expensive that he couldn't afford/buy it.* │

c) He suggested │ *(that) I/she, etc. (should) put* │ *my/her, etc. luggage* │
   under the seat.

d) In spite │ *of his good salary*   │ he was unhappy in his job.
   │ *of (his) earning a good salary*
   │ *having*
   │ *getting*
   │ *of the fact that he earned a good salary* │

e) He objected │ *to* │ *his secretary('s) coming*   │ late to work.
   │ *the fact that his secretary came* │

f) I wish │ *I hadn't missed*   │ your birthday party.
   │ *I had not missed*
   │ *I had attended*
   │ *I had been at*
   │ *I had gone to* │

g) The streets │ *have not* │ *been cleaned* │ this week.
   │ *haven't*

h) Apples are not usually │ *as expensive/dear as* │ oranges.
   │ *so expensive/dear as* │

i) You'd │ *better put*   │ your money in the bank.
   │ *do better to put*
   │ *do better putting* │

j) It is such │ *a dirty restaurant* │ that no one wants to eat there.

Question 3
a) time
b) made/worn/polished
c) hearted
d) aged
e) made/baked

Question 4
a) go over/through
b) goes out/has gone out
c) gone off/sour
d) gone down
e) go in for/have gone in for

Question 5
(1) When does the next flight leave? etc.
(2) Are there any seats available? etc.
(3) What is the first-class fare? etc.
(4) Can I have two first-class tickets? etc.
(5) When can I collect them? etc.
(6) How can I get to the airport? etc.

Question 6
Step one

Identify task – what are they each reading?

Step two

Identify their interests.
These are underlined on the sample pages (pp. 160–1).

Step three

Match interests with magazines.
These are marked with initials on the sample pages.

SAMPLE PAGE (see p. 159)

6   *The following four people are travelling on a train, reading different newspapers or magazines. Using the information given, continue paragraphs 1–4 on page 69 in about 50 words each.*

MB

Name	Age	Family	Job	Interests
Mary Brown	45	Married. 2 children, John (garage mechanic) Sandra (at Secretarial College).	Assistant in dress shop.	Making clothes for herself and daughter. Knitting. Collecting pictures of the Queen which she sticks into a book. Gossiping with friends about television and film stars.

JM

James Moore | 52 | Married. 2 sons, both in family business. | Buying and selling houses. | Anything to do with making money. Owns large country house and likes buying things to make it more beautiful. Shooting and fishing.

FS

Frank Smith | 23 | Single. Lives with parents in small town. | Railway clerk. | Football and swimming. Spends summer holidays in Spain and Portugal near hot, sandy beaches. Likes spending his evenings with his friends and going to discos.

AJ

Anne Jones | 28 | Recently married to a biologist. | College lecturer. | Playing the piano. Going to opera and concerts. Active member of local political group. Likes discussing woman's place in the modern world. Entertaining friends to dinner.

JM

People's Daily	Economic News	MODERN SOCIETY	POPULAR OPINION
★Sandra's Friend the Elephant	Pound/Dollar—Latest fears	—Zambia-Progress Report ?	Royal Babies —delightful picture series
FS—★Disco Beat Latest (Mick's new album)	Investment Advice	—Secretary or Career Woman?	On with the Old Love —Patricia explains
FS—★Win your next great Mediterranean sun holiday	This week's special features on	—Chopin Festival	Fashion at your fingertips —useful ideas
FS—★3 pages of Sports news	COUNTRY SPORTS ANTIQUE FURNITURE	—International Cookery Series— Part 14	

MB

? stars

JM   **AJ**   **MB**

SAMPLE PAGE

(1) I think Mary Brown is reading *Popular Opinion.* First, there are pictures of Royal Babies in it, which she can put in her scrapbook. It also has practical fashion ideas for her to use when she is making clothes. 'The Old Love' may include the sort of gossip she enjoys.

(2) James Moore has chosen *Economic News* because it is concerned with money, which is his main interest. It also has an article on the sort of furniture he probably likes, and the country sports feature probably includes his leisure activities, shooting and fishing.

(3) Frank Smith prefers *People's Daily* because it has an article on a new disco album and that is his favourite sort of music. Also, the sports news probably includes football and swimming, which he likes. Lastly, there's a chance he might win himself a holiday!

(4) Anne Jones is the sort of woman who reads *Modern Society* because it has information on her serious interests such as music, politics and women's careers. She might also get ideas for one of her dinner parties from the cookery series.

Step four

Make notes.

<u>Notes</u>

MB   <u>Pop. Op.</u> because of pics of R. babies – Queen – Fashion ideas

          Old Love ? perhaps film stars

JM   <u>Eco. News</u> because money, investment

                 also his home & leisure

FS   <u>P. Daily</u> because info. about new disco album

          Also sports news probably includes f. & sw.

          Might win holiday.

AJ   <u>Mod. Soc.</u> has info on serious interests

            e.g. politics (Zambia) & woman's place

           & on music (Chopin) & perhaps idea

           for din. party

Step five

Complete the paragraphs.
(See the sample pages, pp. 160–1.)

PAPER 4   LISTENING COMPREHENSION

FIRST PART

A police street interview
1 E
  G

SECOND PART

An Ansafone message
2 867936
3 (hot) (water) tap (in bathroom)
4 annoyed/angry/cross/irritable/upset/impatient
5 (broken) window
6 call (round)/go and see him/come round
7 769823
8 apologize/say (she was/is) sorry for
9 to paint/painting (the outside of) her house
10 230987
11 482194
12 ring/telephone/phone/call/contact
13 (central) heating/(gas) boiler
14 64

THIRD PART

Holiday interviews
15 Yes
16 C
17 B
18 C
19 C
20 Yes
21 C
22 C

TAPESCRIPT

> The rubric on this cassette follows exactly the wording of the
> Cambridge First Certificate Exam. To save space on the cassette
> the repeats have not been included. At the beginning of each
> passage, set the counter on your cassette player to zero. At the
> end of the passage, rewind the cassette to zero to hear the
> passage again. **Remember, you should hear each passage twice
> only!**

Cambridge First Certificate Listening Test

TEST NUMBER 3

You will be given a question paper for First Certificate Test 3.
Your supervisor will give you further instructions. On the
question paper you will see spaces for your name and index
number, and questions for each part of the test. Each part of the
test will be heard twice. There will be pauses to allow you to
look through the questions before each part, and other pauses
to let you think about your answers. At the end of every pause
you will hear this sound.

tone

The tape will now be stopped while question papers are given
out. You must ask any questions now, as you will not be
allowed to speak during the test.

pause

First Part
You will hear a woman talking to a policeman about a robbery
at an electrical shop. Put a tick in the boxes next to the two men
she describes.

pause

tone

> ★TONE★ Set the counter on your cassette player to zero now.

POLICE STREET INTERVIEW

Policeman: Excuse me, madam. (*Yes?*) I'm sorry to trouble

you. You must have heard about the smash and
grab raid last night. We're looking (*Oh, yes*) for
any information that we can get from passers-by,
so, er, have you heard anything?

Woman: Well, erm, I saw a couple of lads last night. I did
think, well, I'm not sure, erm, it's not of any
importance actually because . . .

Policeman: Oh, did you madam? Were they near Robinsons?

Woman: Er, well, yes, they was. That's the electrical place,
isn't it?

Policeman: Could you give me a description of these lads?

Woman: Well, er, um, it's difficult, isn't it?

Policeman: There were two of them, were there?

Woman: Yes, yes, there was two of them. (*I see*) Erm, come
to think of it, oh, it's hard to remember what they
looked like.

Policeman: How tall were they?

Woman: Now. I do remember one of them. Now, let me see
now. I'm 162 cms and I suppose one of them was   1st man
about 180 cms and the other one was very short. I
do remember 'cause they looked so funny
together. One was about 160 cms and the other   2nd man
one was about 180 cms and the very short one,
well he had long greasy hair right down to his   2nd man
shoulders. (*Yes, Madam*) You know punk and now,
now I'm almost sure that he was wearing a leather   2nd man
jacket.

Policeman: A leather jacket?

Woman: Yes, oh yes, and it had things on the back and I
don't know what they was.

Policeman: Decorated were they, madam?

Woman: Yes, it was, and, er, jeans . . .

Policeman: Like a, like a motorcycle rider's then, madam?

Woman: Yes, it was, and very greasy his hair was I can
remember that, you know, punk.

Policeman: Was it dark hair? (*Eh?*) Could you see the colour of
their hair, madam?

Woman: Colour? Yes, very greasy dark hair.   2nd man

Policeman: I see and how about the taller one, the man you   1st man
say was about 180 cms?

Woman: Oh, now he had very short hair. It was cut really
short I'd say and he had, he had on this sweater   1st man
'cause it was quite cold last night and he didn't
have a jacket on. (*I see, yes I see*) Oh, and he had a
tattoo. Now I remember he had a tattoo on his   1st man
arm.

Policeman: Can you describe the tattoo at all madam?

Woman: No, no I can't, because it was dark, you see, and I didn't really pay much attention, but I do remember thinking, 'Well, now I wonder what they're doing?' You see?

Policeman: I see, madam.

Woman: You see? In the doorway there over there, because I was stood there waiting for my friend to come down from the nightclub (*I see, yes*) you know, where she's working there, you know, in the Ladies' Toilets there, so I was stood there for quite a few minutes and they was just standing, standing, there. Well . . . looking suspicious, really, I suppose . . .

Policeman: Do you think they saw you, madam?

Woman: Oh yes. Oh yes. I'm sure they did.

Policeman: And at about what time would this be?

pause

tone

Now you will hear the piece again.

★★TONE★★   Rewind the cassette to zero to hear the passage a second time.

---

pause

That is the end of the first part of the test.

pause

Second Part

In the second part of the test you will hear a telephone answering machine. For questions 2–14 fill in the missing information in the spaces provided.

pause

tone

★TONE★   Set the counter on your cassette player to zero now.

ANSAFONE

Mrs Curry: Hello, er, yes, this is Mrs Betty Curry here, I'm ringing about my hot water tap in the bathroom. I can't turn it off, so it means I've had to turn off everything, the whole supply, you see. So now I haven't got any water at all. So, er, could you ring me and arrange a time to come and fix it? My number is 867936. That's 867936. Er, thank you. — Q3, Q2

Mr Harris: Ah, yes. This is Harris here, John Harris. I keep ringing you, but you always seem to be out, and you haven't rung back even though I've left my name and number. Er, please ring this time. I've got a broken window, which the child next door put a football through, as I said last time I rang. So I want it mended, please, because it's cold, and the rain's getting in. Now, my phone's not working either. I'm ringing from a public phone. But you can either call round or ring my neighbour and leave a message with her. That's, erm, Mrs Irene Jenkins, and her telephone is 769823, 769823. Oh, and, my address again, though you should have it, is 49 Grantham Close, the bungalow on the corner. Thanks. — Q4, Q5, Q6, Q7

Miss Embury: Yes, um, this is Miss Embury here. Er, 20 Trent Road. I'm ringing to apologize for not being here when you called round. I had to go out unexpectedly, and when I got back, you'd already been. As I said when I phoned last time, I want you to estimate the cost of painting the outside of my house. So maybe, now you've seen the house, you could tell me the cost over the phone, or ring me to make another appointment. My number is 230987. 230987. Goodbye. — Q8, Q9, Q10

Mr Grant: Ah, this is Grant here. 64 Station Avenue. I, I wonder if you could ring me back about my central heating. You came and had a look at it, if you remember, last week, because it was smelling of gas round the boiler. Well, I'm afraid it's started again. If anything, it's worse. And when the boiler lights, it goes bang, er, quite loudly. It's pretty urgent. Oh, my phone number is 482194. Goodbye. — Q14, Q12, Q13, Q11

pause

tone

Now you will hear the piece again.

WHERE THE
CLUES ARE

★★TONE★★ Rewind the cassette to zero to hear the passage a
second time.

---

pause

That is the end of the second part of the test.

pause

Third Part
You will hear some people talking about holidays. For
questions 15–19, tick the boxes that correspond to the man's
answers. For questions 20–22, tick the boxes which correspond
to the woman's answers.

pause

tone

★TONE★ Set the counter on your cassette player to zero now.

HOLIDAYS

Interviewer:	Do you go away for your summer holidays at all?	
Man:	Yes, yes I do.	
Interviewer:	Oh, where?	
Man:	Yes, usually abroad.	Q15
Interviewer:	Whereabouts did you go last year?	
Man:	Last year um . . . Majorca actually.	Q16
Interviewer:	How long did you go for?	
Man:	A fortnight . . .	Q17
Interviewer:	. . . and you enjoyed it?	
Man:	Yes, very much so. We went to, er, to the north-ern part of the island and it was very pleasant.	
Interviewer:	Nice to get some sunny weather . . .	
Man:	Yes, very hot actually, very, very hot.	
Interviewer:	Where do you think you're going this year?	
Man:	This year, um, I'm going to wait actually to book later in the spring and decide at fairly short notice.	Q18
Interviewer:	What usually governs where you go, what kind of thing?	

Man:	Well, er, usually my fiancée likes to fly off some- where, so that's er, one of the criteria, so it equates with going abroad, er, so that's the main thing I think, so it'll probably be abroad again this year somewhere in Europe.	WHERE THE CLUES ARE ↓
Interviewer:	And, er, what about the exchange rates at the moment, the pound's not very good value over- seas, does that – will that bother you at all?	
Man:	Not really, er, I think the fluctuations are rela- tively so small that if you're going to have a holiday you'll probably go regardless.	
Interviewer:	And, um, does anything else govern your choice of holiday apart from all that?	
Man:	Oh, um, the ultimate cost obviously, I noticed this year looking through brochures that holi- days have gone up, but I'm sure it won't put us off totally.	
Interviewer:	You feel you deserve a holiday, do you?	Q19
Man:	That's right, absolutely.	
Woman:	Last year we got scorched in Norfolk and soaked in Woolacombe.	
Interviewer:	Oh, well, tell me what happened?	
Woman:	Well, in Norfolk we were expecting it to be cold and blustery and it turned out to be an absolute heatwave and then in Woolacombe where we were expecting the sun and the sea and the sand, it rained solidly for a week!	
Interviewer:	Oh dear! But you did enjoy it?	Q20
Woman:	Oh yes, yes it was good fun.	
Interviewer:	And what are you planning to do this year?	
Woman:	Ah, this year, well I have no plans at the moment. Perhaps Greece in late September but nothing at the moment.	Q21
Interviewer:	What usually governs your choice of destination for a holiday?	
Woman:	Well, er, well, they are usually on a whim, my holidays are arranged a week before I go usually, so, well, I prefer holidays like that.	Q22
Interviewer:	You don't want to start planning it in January and think about it all through the year?	
Woman:	Oh, no, no, no.	

pause

tone

Now you will hear the piece again.

★★TONE★★ Rewind the cassette to zero to hear the passage a second time.

---

pause

That is the end of the third part of the test.

There will now be a pause to allow you to check your work. The question papers will then be collected by your supervisor.

pause

tone

That is the end of the test.

Key to Practice Test 4

PAPER 1   READING COMPREHENSION

SECTION A

(See Study Notes p. 8 for Suggested method of working.)

1   B   *view*
    Meaning: You can see the mountains clearly.
    Distractor check:
    A   *vision*   God appeared to him in a vision.
    C   *sight*   We had nearly run out of petrol when we saw the garage: it was a very welcome sight.
    D   *picture*   There's a picture of the mountains hanging on the wall of my room.

2   C   *any†*
    Meaning: I'm completely out of change.
    Distractor check:
    A   *some*   The bank certainly has some change.
    B   *lots*   The bank certainly has lots of change.
    D   *all*   This train doesn't go any further. All change!

3   B   *is†*
    Meaning: I hope it is going to be fine, because I want to go out later.
    (Note: check Conditional structures in your reference grammar.)
    Distractor check:
    A   *was*   If it was fine, I would go out. (But it isn't, so I can't.)
    C   *were*   If it were fine, I would go out. (But it isn't, so I can't.)
    D   *will be*   The forecast says it will be fine tomorrow.

4   D   *plenty†*
    Meaning: We've lots of time before the train goes, so we don't have to hurry.
    Distractor check:
    A   *very much*   We haven't very much time.
    B   *enough*   We've enough time.
    C   *great deal*   We've a great deal of time.

† This is correct because it fits the structure of the sentence as well as the meaning.

5 B *out*†
    Meaning: Things are not at all clear to me.
    Distractor check:
    A *away*   The burglars made away with all the jewellery.
    C *do*   There isn't any real coffee. We'll have to make do with instant coffee.
    D *over*   He made all his money over to his children before he died.

6 D *forgetful*†
    Meaning: He never remembers things.
    Distractor check:
    A *forgetting*   He is always forgetting things.
    B *forgotten*   He has forgotten to bring his book.
    C *forgettable*   Don't bother to read that book. The story is very forgettable.

7 C *taking*
    Meaning: Don't take risks on the road.
    Distractor check:
    A *putting*   His heavy drinking is putting his whole career at risk.
    B *setting*   My boss is always setting me impossible tasks to do.
    D *being*   Look at the way he's driving! He's being very careless!

8 D *would have come*†
    Meaning: We didn't know it, so we didn't come.
    Distractor check:
    A *came*   We knew your address, so we came to see you.
    B *will come*   If you tell us your address, we will come to see you.
    C *would come*   If we knew your address, we would come to see you. (But we don't know it, so we can't.)

9 D *group*
    Meaning: There were several of them.
    Distractor check:
    A *gang*   That gang of youths terrorizes the whole street.
    B *crowd*   A small crowd of demonstrators was waiting for the President to arrive.
    C *team*   Two of my students are in the school football team.

10 B *alike*†
    Meaning: It's difficult to know which is which.
    Distractor check:
    A *likeness*   That painting of her is a very good likeness.
    C *same*   See you next week – same time, same place! (Note: 'same'

† This is correct because it fits the structure of the sentence as well as the meaning.

without definite article is always colloquial.)
D   *the same*   Our two cars are the same make.

11 D   *post†*
    Meaning: He went there to look for a job as a teacher.
    Distractor check:
A   *work*   He went to find work as a teacher.
B   *occupation*   'What is your occupation?' 'I'm a teacher.'
C   *employment*   He went to find employment as a teacher.

12 A   *then*
    Meaning: First we'll play tennis, and after that we'll have lunch. (Note:
    'afterwards' would also be acceptable.)
    Distractor check:
B   *straight away*   . . . and afterwards we'll have lunch straight away.
C   *immediately*   . . . and immediately afterwards we'll have lunch.
D   *so*   I won the game, so he had to pay for lunch.

13 D   *remembered†*
    Meaning: The bread is almost finished, so it's important that he
    doesn't forget to buy some.
    Distractor check:
A   *reminded*   I telephoned and reminded him to buy some bread.
B   *proposed*   I proposed that we should have sandwiches during the
    meeting, to save time.
C   *suggested*   The shops were closed, so he suggested that we should
    bake some bread ourselves.
    or . . . he suggested baking some bread ourselves.

14 C   *refused†*
    Meaning: He said 'no'.
    Distractor check:
A   *objected*   He objected to being questioned.
B   *denied*   He denied stealing the money.
D   *disliked*   He probably disliked the police.

15 D   *off*
    Meaning: Leave the bus at Forest Road.
    Distractor check:
A   *up*   I get up at 7.00 a.m.
B   *down*   The cat couldn't get down from the top of the tree.
C   *outside*   Quick! Get outside! There's a bomb in here!

† This is correct because it fits the structure of the sentence as well as the meaning.

16 C   *point*†
         Meaning: It's useless to go to school if you don't want to learn.
         Distractor check:
    A   *reason*   Having a cold is no reason for not going to school. (Note:
         compare 'cause'.)
    B   *aim*   What is your aim in going on this expedition?
    D   *purpose*   What is the purpose of going to school?

17 B   *bitterly*
         Meaning: The way that she complained showed that she felt she was
         being treated very unfairly indeed.
         Distractor check:
    A   *severely*   She was severely injured in the crash.
    C   *extremely*   She was extremely upset by the news.
    D   *terribly*   She was terribly upset by the news.

18 C   *pain*†
         Meaning: He was not free from the pain for a long time.
         Distractor check:
    A   *hurt*   He hurt his back in a car accident.
    B   *ache*   I've got a terrible ache in my shoulder. (Note: 'ache' is always
         countable, but 'backache' can be uncountable!)
    D   *injury*   The injury to his back gave him a lot of trouble.

19 A   *told*†
         Meaning: He gave me directions.
         Distractor check:
    B   *said*   He said he didn't know the way.
    C   *explained*   He explained the way to me very clearly.
    D   *directed*   He directed me to where I wanted to go.

20 C   *woven*†
         Meaning: It was made of silk.
         Distractor check:
    A   *composed*   The class is composed of three Japanese, two Saudis and
         five Germans.
    B   *worn*   This dress has only been worn once.
    D   *threaded*   He threaded the needle and mended the hole in his sock.

21 C   *in the middle*†
         Meaning: She had done some of the work but not all of it.
         Distractor check:
    A   *at the centre*   She was at the centre of a political scandal.
    B   *on her way*   She was on her way to the kitchen when the phone rang.

† This is correct because it fits the structure of the sentence as well as the meaning.

D   *halfway through*   She was halfway through making a cake when we
    arrived.

22 C   *Unless*
        Meaning: You'll only pass if you do better work than this.
        Distractor check:
    A   *Although*   Although he worked hard, he failed the exam.
    B   *If*   If you work hard, you'll pass.
    D   *When*   When you take the exam, try not to feel nervous.

23 C   *fill in*
        Meaning: You have to write the necessary information in the
        appropriate places on the form.
        Distractor check:
    A   *make up*   Get the things together, and make them up into a parcel.
    B   *write down*   Write down the reasons you want to join the Music
        Society.
    D   *do up*   Do up the parcel with string before you send it off.

24 D   *in†*
        Meaning: Chemistry was the subject of the examination.
        Distractor check:
    A   *on*   There were two questions on metallic elements.
    B   *about*   I don't know much about chemistry.
    C   *for*   I'm revising for an examination.

25 D   *anyone†*
        Meaning: They would like any person who saw the accident to contact
        them.
        Distractor check:
    A   *somebody*   They've spoken to somebody who saw the accident.
    B   *someone*   They've spoken to someone who saw the accident.
    C   *one*   They've spoken to one man who saw the accident.

SECTION B

FIRST PASSAGE

26 C
    because
    They prefer 'rough open country'. (paragraph 1, line 3)
    Distractor check:

† This is correct because it fits the structure of the sentence as well as the meaning.

A   There are no snakes in Ireland.
B   Adders are the only snake in Scotland – but that's not the same thing.
D   Adders prefer the sun, not the shade.

27   B
because
Most attempts are either unnecessary or unwise. (paragraph 2)
Distractor check:
A   You'll probably end up getting bitten yourself!
C   Snake bites can kill!
D   Do-it-yourself surgery can be dangerous.

28   B
because
They will attack only if they feel threatened. (paragraph 3, lines 3–5)
Distractor check:
A   They're frightened of people.
C   They get out of the way if they hear you coming.
D   The text says the opposite.

29   A
because
It would rather avoid you. (paragraph 3, lines 5–6)
Distractor check:
B   Read the sentence 'If it hears you coming . . .' (paragraph 3, lines 5–7)
C   Adders can't move very quickly.
D   If it had a chance to avoid you, it would.

30   C
because
The aim of the passage is to correct this misapprehension.
Distractor check:
A   We aren't told what they think about this.
B   Most people think a snake bite is 'a fatal misfortune'. (paragraph 2, line 1)
D   As above, most people think a snake bite is 'a fatal misfortune'. (paragraph 2, line 1)

SECOND PASSAGE

31   A
because
A single union can affect a large area of the economy. (paragraph 2, lines 1–3)
Distractor check:

B   The text doesn't say this.
C   They have a larger membership – but that's not the same thing.
D   True – but it doesn't answer the question.

32 B
because
A single industry may involve many unions. (paragraph 2, lines 6–9)
Distractor check:
A   These industries are not the problem.
C   55 per cent is a high number, not a low one.
D   The text doesn't give this as a reason.

33 A
because
Several examples are given in the third paragraph.
Distractor check:
B   Their problem is losing existing members, not getting new ones.
C   The problem with new technologies is that of rejection, not of learning.
D   The text does not mention this.

34 C
because
' . . . the jobs of other unions' members are threatened . . .' (paragraph 3,
line 8)
Distractor check:
A   The problem of representation applies only to new trades.
B   The text doesn't mention this.
D   The text doesn't mention this.

35 B
because
They both have 'problems of internal communication just as managers do'.
(paragraph 4, lines 1–2)
Distractor check:
A   The text doesn't mention this.
C   This may be true, but the text doesn't say so.
D   This may be true too, but the text doesn't say so.

36 B
because
Most of the problems described in the text spring from this.
Distractor check:
A   This is not mentioned as a problem.
C   We are not told about 'employers' organizations'.
D   It says that Britain has very high union membership.

THIRD PASSAGE

37 B
    because
    It'll be the first one the computer selects. (paragraph 7)
    Distractor check:
    A   But we are told the closing date, so we know the winner is selected
         from all the correct entries received by then.
    C   You can send your entry before then if you want.
    D   No, the first one.

38 B
    because
    It asks for the name *of the track*.
    (The answers are: Brunel, Amy Johnson, Mary Queen of Scots and Brands
    Hatch.)
    Distractor check:
    A   We cannot know this from the text.
    C   It's near a *motor racing track*; we are not told how easy it is to reach.
    D   That's question 1, not question 4.

39 B
    because
    You can choose either a traditional lunch or a packed lunch in addition to
    the dinner.
    Distractor check:
    A   To stay free, children have to share a room with their parents.
    C   There is lunch on one day only.
    D   There is no suggestion it is served in the guest's room, and a *full*
         English breakfast doesn't sound very light, does it?

40 D
    because
    It's their only recommendation.
    Distractor check:
    A   You don't need to enter the competition to get a booklet.
    B   You need the booklet first, to get the addresses.
    C   That's the address for competition entries.

PAPER 2   COMPOSITION

NOTES

(These notes may be consulted at various stages in your work. See Study Notes p. 11.)

1

Task Check

You must mention – that you can't go
– the explanation for this
– the present you are sending

Register Check

Informal – this is a friend, not your boss.

Technique

If you haven't written this sort of letter for a while, look up in a reference book the rules for setting out an informal letter.

DANGER! Do not begin letters in English with 'Hello!', even very informal ones. Always use 'Dear . . .'
Never begin 'Dear friend'. You should use your friend's name or nickname.

Sample Plan

para 1 – apologies & regrets

para 2 – reason

Note: reason must be strong, probably not illness, because wedding invitations usually sent out well before the date; could be unalterable travel plans, exam date, job interview, etc.

para 3 – the present (what it is, why chosen, its use, or pleasure I hope they'll get from it, etc.)

Note: you must mention you are sending the present – perhaps you'll make something of this, it could be large or heavy or fragile, being sent by special delivery, etc.

para 4 – repeat regrets, love/regards to the family & fiancé (e)

2

Task Check

– It's a place, not necessarily a building, so anywhere that might be interesting to tourists (a picturesque fishing port, a factory producing a local speciality food or drink, a craft workshop, modern shopping precinct – as long as it can be in a city)
– You're a tourist guide, so you must know a lot about the place, not just be able to describe it
– Tell them about the history of the place, the people working or living there, why it's special, and what tourists can do there
– Nobody's going to check your facts, only your language, so you could possibly invent a place, or write about somewhere you've never seen, but be careful, this is a trick which needs practice!

Register Check

Slightly formal, you're in a professional role, but the audience consists of people on holiday, so be friendly. Remember you're speaking, not writing.

Technique

List the facts you want to mention, then plan your paragraphs. Number the facts for each paragraph and think about the vocabulary you need. Have a clear picture of the audience in your mind as you write, always be talking to them.

DANGER! Don't spend much time on description, remember your audience will be able to see it for themselves.

Sample Plan

Shopping Centre

a) LIST
built 1892–3, replaced derelict factory, won prize for architecture (note: unusual windows in roof), 2 department stores, also small shops (note: local hand-made shoes). Also specialist bakers, Japanese restaurant (expensive but good). Museum of local history. All indoors, air-conditioned, no stairs (good for disabled shoppers), people come from as far away as 50 kms to shop for electrical goods, cameras, etc. Excellent coffee shop with traditional local cakes.

---

b) PLAN

para 1 – introduce self, welcome, say what I'm going to talk about

para 2 – background, history of place, describe briefly (remind them to look at windows)

para 3 – reasons why local people like it

para 4 – special points for tourists

para 5 – time of tour, hope they enjoy it, etc.

3

Task Check
It's a dream, anything's possible BUT it must be unpleasant in some way because you're relieved that it was only a dream. (It could be a terrible interview, or being late for an exam, for example.) Opportunity to introduce comedy, if you can handle the language.

Register Check
Informal narrative, to match the final sentence.

Technique
Plan a simple story in quite a lot of detail, organizing each part into a paragraph, and stick to your plan. Think carefully about words you will need to use.

DANGER! Don't get so excited about inventing fantastic events that you forget to control your language. This sort of task can be much more difficult than you'd expect.

4

Task Check
– The subject is computers *and* other machines
– The trend is assumed to be a fact by the title
– You must describe your feelings about this trend, giving reasons for your opinion

Register Check
Fairly formal – take your tone from the title.

Technique
Gather your ideas (brainstorm?), then organize them into pros and cons, with examples, to show how you reach your opinion.

DANGER! Don't spend a lot of time describing the changes taking place in the modern world rather than giving your opinion. Just offer short examples to support your argument.

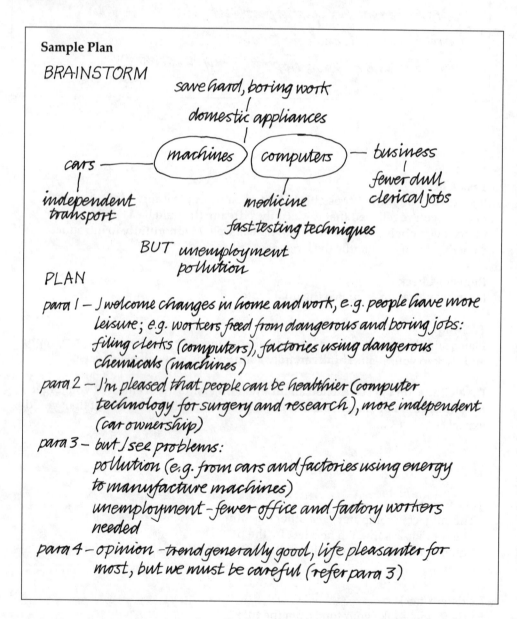

Sample Plan

BRAINSTORM

save hard, boring work

domestic appliances

cars ——— (machines)(computers) — business

independent   fewer dull
transport   medicine   clerical jobs

fast testing techniques

BUT unemployment
pollution

PLAN

para 1 — I welcome changes in home and work, e.g. people have more
leisure; e.g. workers freed from dangerous and boring jobs:
filing clerks (computers), factories using dangerous
chemicals (machines)

para 2 — I'm pleased that people can be healthier (computer
technology for surgery and research), more independent
(car ownership)

para 3 — but I see problems:
pollution (e.g. from cars and factories using energy
to manufacture machines)
unemployment - fewer office and factory workers
needed

para 4 — opinion - trend generally good, life pleasanter for
most, but we must be careful (refer para 3)

PAPER 3 USE OF ENGLISH

Question 1

1	for	11	tree
2	in	12	the/this
3	had	13	reached
4	away/ahead	14	there/here
5	which	15	do
6	heard	16	glad/relieved/happy/pleased/thankful
7	much/considerably/far	17	Finally/Eventually/Ultimately
8	than	18	away/off
9	well/clearly/distinctly	19	could
10	did	20	completely/totally/utterly/quite/absolutely

Common error check:

1 at ✗

You cannot look *at* something unless you know it is there. The writer did not say *the/some* rabbits, so we know he meant 'rabbits in general'. e.g. I was looking at some rabbits which I wanted to draw. *Also,* he would probably stand still to look at some rabbits, not walk along, or they'd run away!

4 far ✗

'Far' cannot be used in this structure. Note: It is correct at 7, because it means 'much' in that context.

Question 2

a) If | *he does not phone* / *he doesn't phone* | immediately he won't get any information.

b) When | *did they buy the house?* |

c) The broken vase | *could not be* / *couldn't be* | *repaired.* |

d) The garden hasn't | *(yet) been* | *dug.* |

e) Is this | *the cheapest carpet* / *the cheapest one* | *you've got* / *you have* | ? |

f) These shoes | *are too small* / *are not big enough* | for my feet.

g) I am looking │ *forward* │ *to meeting* │ you.
                            │ *to seeing* │

h) The security guard told │ *us* │ *to keep away* │ from this area, when we
approached the fence.

i) It's │ *the first time* │ *I have (ever) met* │ such a famous person.
                          │ *I've (ever) met*   │

j) You don't │ *have to* │ take this pudding out of its tin to cook it.
             │ *need to* │

Question 3
a) success
b) victory
c) loosen
d) fresh
e) melts

Question 4
a) put up with
b) putting off
c) putting on
d) Put (your toys) away

Question 5
(1) How long is the path? etc.
(2) I can't walk that far! etc.
(3) Do I need walking boots?
(4) Is it easy to get lost? etc.
(5) What is there to see? etc.
(6) How much are they? etc.
(7) I'll take them both. etc.

Question 6
Step one

Identify task – how should each person travel?

Step two

Identify main facts about each person's journey.
(These are noted on the sample page, p. 186.)

Step three

Make notes.

NOTES
<u>NOTES</u>

P.S. <u>mustn't</u> be late
               be tired
               get lost
       cost no problem

A.C. must be able to walk ? move
       no car
       money ?

J.N. 2 adults + 2 children — ? cost
       no hurry
       knows the way ?   ? get bored
       has car

M.S. not much time
       ? money
       no car

Step four

Check illustration and notes to decide how they should travel.
Note: This is your opinion – any choice can be correct if it is supported by the
facts provided.

Step five

Complete the paragraphs.
(See the sample page, p. 187.)

SAMPLE PAGE (see p. 184)

6 *Study the illustration showing the cost and journey time of different ways of travelling from London to Manchester, and the notes below. Complete the paragraphs on page 88 in the spaces provided, explaining which way you think each person should travel in winter when the weather is bad. (You may choose any way for any person, provided you give reasons.)*

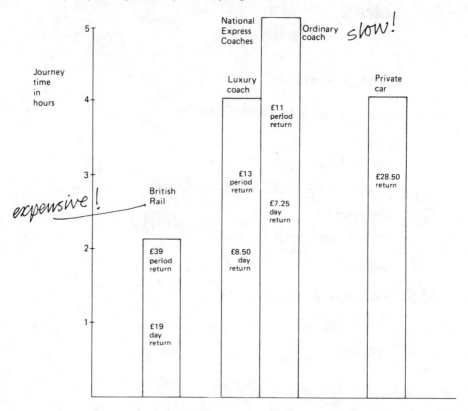

London – Manchester: journey times and fares.

Notes

1. Day return ticket – you must go and come back the <u>same</u> day.

2. Period return ticket – you can go and come back up to three months later.

3. Luxury coaches have reclining seats, toilets, food and drink, hostesses, and video films. Ordinary coaches have none of these.   *+time is shorter*

4. The cost of the car journey includes all the costs of running a car, not just petrol costs.

5. Students and children can get reductions on trains but not on coaches.

SAMPLE PAGE (see p. 185)

Philip Smith   aged 23. He needs to go to Manchester, where he has never been before, for an interview for a new job and must be there by 10 a.m. All his expenses will be paid by the the company. He has a car.

I think Philip Smith will go by ...*train (day return)*........... (Cost £ *19*   )

because *the train only takes two hours so he can arrive in time for his interview. The cost does not matter as the company will pay. It's also important that he should arrive fresh and relaxed, but if he goes by car he might get lost and arrive tired and tense, because he doesn't know Manchester.*

Agnes Clark   aged 72. She needs to go to Manchester to look after her sister who has just left hospital. If Agnes sits down for long periods of time, she gets terrible pains in her legs.

In my opinion Agnes Clark will go by *train (period return)* (Cost £ *39*   )

because *She must be able to get up and move about during the journey, otherwise her legs will hurt. It will be rather expensive, but as she has no car, she has no alternative.*

James Norris   aged 42. He is going to Manchester with his wife and two children to spend the Christmas holiday, as usual, with his parents. He has a car.

It would be best for James to travel by *car* .... (Cost £ *28·50*)

because *with two adults and two children this has to be the cheapest way. It probably doesn't matter how long they take as they're going on holiday. They know the route, because they usually go there, and if the children get bored, it'll be easy to take a break.*

Mary Stevens   aged 22. She is going to Manchester to spend the weekend with her boyfriend and his family. She was a student at London University and has just started her first job. She hasn't got a car.

I believe Mary Stevens will choose to go by *luxury coach* (Cost £ *13*   )

because *she's only got the weekend so she'll want to get there quite quickly. On the other hand, she's only just started earning, so paying £ 39 for the train might be rather extravagant.*

PAPER 4   LISTENING COMPREHENSION

FIRST PART

Lona speaking about her life
  1 B
  2 C
  3 C
  4 B

SECOND PART

An old lady's holiday arrangements
  5 Monday or Tuesday
    (after the weekend)
  6 on/on top of
  7 half a/½/a half
  8 (it's) dry
  9 every day/evening/daily
 10 twice/two times/a couple of times/not every day/a couple of days
 11 (electric) light
 12 079448

THIRD PART

Edinburgh Leisureline information
 13 true
 14 true
 15 false
 16 true
 17 true
 18 false
 19 false
 20 false

FOURTH PART

A diary booking being discussed
 21 Heart
 22 assembly hall
 23 screen

TAPESCRIPT

> The rubric on this cassette follows exactly the wording of the
> Cambridge First Certificate Exam. To save space on the cassette
> the repeats have not been included. At the beginning of each
> passage, set the counter on your cassette player to zero. At the
> end of the passage, rewind the cassette to zero to hear the
> passage again. **Remember, you should hear each passage twice
> only!**

Cambridge First Certificate Listening Test

TEST NUMBER 4

You will be given a question paper for First Certificate Test 4.
Your supervisor will give you further instructions. On the
question paper you will see spaces for your name and index
number, and questions for each part of the test. Each part of the
test will be heard twice. There will be pauses to allow you to
look through the questions before each part, and other pauses
to let you think about your answers. At the end of every pause
you will hear this sound.

tone

The tape will now be stopped while question papers are given
out. You must ask any questions now, as you will not be
allowed to speak during the test.

pause

First Part
You will hear a woman talking about her family and interests.
For questions 1 to 4 tick one of the boxes A, B, C or D.

pause

tone

> ★TONE★ Set the counter on your cassette player to zero now.

'LONA'

Hello, everyone. I'm Lona and I'm going to tell you a little bit
about myself and my interests.

I was born in North Carolina and at an early age moved to
Virginia where I grew up on a dairy farm. I'm in my thirties,   Q1
married, and have a young daughter, Shannon, aged six.
Presently I am a teacher at the elementary school at Indian
Harbour Beach, Florida, where I teach fourth grade, er, which is
boys and girls aged nine and ten years old. I attended school at
Virginia Polytechnic Institute in Blacksberg, Virginia, where I
met my husband who was a senior engineering student. When I
have free time from caring for my daughter and my household, I
like to read. Mainly I'm interested in reading English History   Q2
and American Civil War stories, although I like to read historical fiction stories as well, about the old South or about Kings
and Queens of England from long ago. Also I like to sew and do
needlework, especially crewel embroidery and county cross
stitch which is quite a challenge for anyone. Travelling is a
hobby that my husband and I both enjoy. Perhaps we've seen   Q3
more in the United Kingdom than we have in the United States,
but we intend to change that in a few years – take our daughter
to see the West coast of the United States, where I've not even
been.
    When we leave the United States, we next want to take a trip
to Switzerland and Austria, because this is a place that I have
dreamed about since I was a young child in school.
    The important thing in our life in Florida is that we enjoy
having no snow. When my husband and I were both natives of
Virginia and we grew up, we remember having to miss so many
days of school for snow and ice and sleet, so it was a nice
change for us to move to Florida about 16 years ago, where we
enjoy the mild climate in the wintertime and we also enjoy
swimming and tennis and boating. However, I must say that I
still do miss the change of seasons and as long as I shall live in
Florida and enjoy Florida I will also still miss the springtime   Q4
flowers and the leaves falling in the Fall.

pause

tone

Now you will hear the piece again.

TONE Rewind the cassette to zero to hear the passage a
second time.

---

pause

That is the end of the first part of the test.

pause

190

Second Part
You will hear a conversation between an old lady and her
neighbour. For questions 5–12, fill in the missing information
in the gaps provided.

pause

tone

★TONE★ Set the counter on your cassette player to zero now.

HOLIDAY ARRANGEMENTS

Old lady:	Oh hello, dear. Come in.
Young woman:	No, I've only got a moment. I just wanted to check, um, exactly what is it you want me to do when you're away next week? When is it you're actually leaving?
Old lady:	Well, I'm going about midday on Tuesday.
Young woman:	Yeah, and when will you be back?
Old lady:	After the weekend, Monday or Tuesday.
Young woman:	So it'll be about a week altogether? Right. Er, now, what about the cat? Er, I don't have to let her in or out, do I?
Old lady:	Oh no, no, no, she's got a catflap.
Young woman:	Yeah, so, er, she can come and go as she pleases . . .
Old lady:	Yes.
Young woman:	And what about her food?
Old lady:	Well, I've left some tins of catfood on top. Well, I shall do, on top of the fridge (*Mm*). And a tin-opener, and give her about half a tin a day, (*What half a . . .?*) half in the morning, half in the evening.
Young woman:	What, so it's a whole tin in a day?
Old lady:	No, no, no. Half a tin a day.
Young woman:	Half of it in the morning and half . . .
Old lady:	In the evening.
Young woman:	OK, yes.
Old lady:	All right.
Young woman:	Now, er, what about the garden? Anything you want me to do?
Old lady:	Well, it depends on the weather.
Young woman:	Ah, what? Watering?
Old lady:	Well, you could water the garden if it's dry . . .
Young woman:	Yeah.

Q5

Q6

Q7

Q8

Old lady:	. . . in any case you could have a look at the tomatoes at the top of the garden . . .	WHERE THE CLUES ARE ↓
Young woman:	Yeah.	
Old lady:	. . . 'cause they will need water anyway . . .	
Young woman:	Yeah. What every day?	Q9
Old lady:	Well, if you have the time . . .	
Young woman:	Yes, I'll do it in the evening.	
Old lady:	Mm, that'll be fine.	
Young woman:	Is there anything in the house?	
Old lady:	Well, there, there are a few houseplants (*Yeah*) you could water those a couple of times while I'm away.	Q10
Young woman:	What, I mean, not every day?	
Old lady:	Oh, no, no . . .	
Young woman:	Um, what about the gas and electricity, are they switched off?	
Old lady:	Well, the gas'll be turned off but I shall leave the electricity on (*Mmhm*) and if you wouldn't mind, perhaps, one or two evenings leaving the electric light on and pull the curtains . . .	Q11
Young woman:	Yeah, what, so it looks as if there's . . .	
Old lady:	Somebody . . .	
Young woman:	Mmm . . .	
Old lady:	. . . about.	
Young woman:	Well, because, you know, people do look out for the, they . . . notice. Well, that sounds quite straightforward. What about the key? Will you leave it somewhere hidden?	
Old lady:	Well, you'll be at work so I'll put that in your letterbox when I leave.	
Young woman:	Aha, yeah, OK.	
Old lady:	Will that suit you?	
Young woman:	Yeah, that's fine, and there won't be any other key. Um, so the first time I'll go round will be Tuesday evening?	
Old lady:	Yes. Right.	
Young woman:	I'll probably see you before then, but if I don't I'll go round Tuesday evening. (*Ah*) Um, have you got a phone number you can give me? Just in case I need to contact you?	
Old lady:	Oh, yes, that . . . that'd be a good idea.	
Young woman:	Shall I take it now?	
Young woman:	Yeah? Have you got it?	
Old lady:	Oh, oh, yes, yes.	
Young woman:	All right.	
Old lady:	Um, er, oh-seven-nine-double-four-eight.	Q12

Young woman:	Yeah, OK fine. I'm sure I won't need to use it.	WHERE THE
	Have a good trip, anyway.	CLUES ARE
Old lady:	Oh, thank you very much, dear, and thank	
	you for your kind offer.	↓
Young woman:	That's all right. Bye.	
Old lady:	Goodbye, dear.	

pause

tone

Now you will hear the piece again.

★★TONE★★ Rewind the cassette to zero to hear the passage a
second time.

---

pause

That is the end of the second part of the test.

pause

Third Part

You will hear a recorded telephone announcement for tourists
visiting Edinburgh, Scotland. For questions 13–20, tick whether
the statements are true or false.

pause

tone

★TONE★ Set the counter on your cassette player to zero now.

EDINBURGH LEISURELINE

Welcome to Edinburgh. We have some suggestions for ways in
which you might like to spend your day in and around the   Q13
capital.

Edinburgh Zoo has Scotland's finest collection of wild animals and is open between 9 a.m. and 6 p.m. 365 days a year. The   Q14
largest colony of penguins in any zoo shares a beautiful
parkland setting that includes over 300 different species. Bring
the family and spend the day at the zoo. It's only 15 minutes   Q15
from the city centre. Buses to and from the zoo are numbers 12,
26, 31 and 86. Car parking facilities are also available.

Your entertainment at the Ross Open Air Theatre in Princes
Street Gardens begins today at 3 p.m. with a concert given by

the Regimental Band of the Queen's Own Hussars. From 7 p.m.
John Wilson and his Band provide the music for the Old Time
Dance Championships, 'Come Dancing'.   Q16

The historical Duddingston Kirk beside Duddingston Loch is
open to visitors today. Teas will be served in this twelfth   Q17
century church in the afternoon. It will be open from 10 a.m.
until 6 p.m. today.

One of the best ways to see this beautiful and historic city is
by joining one of the many coach tours organized by Lothian
Regional Transport. These tours cover all parts of the city and
leave from Waverley Bridge, just off Princes Street, throughout
the day. For details, please phone 554 4494.   Q18

Most of Scotland is on Edinburgh's doorstep. You will be
surprised just how much you can see of it in one day. Scottish
Omnibus operate an extensive and varied programme of day
and afternoon tours every day from St Andrew's Square. Phone
556 8464.

If the weather is clear, why not visit the Wellhouse Tower and
Camera Obscura at the top of the Royal Mile near Edinburgh
Castle? Here, you can look out on magnificent views of Edinburgh and beyond, through this unique optical device installed
in 1850. There is also a Scottish gift, book and record shop.
The Camera Obscura is open every day between 9.30 a.m. and   Q19
5 p.m.

For your entertainment in the theatre this evening, the King's
Theatre in Leven Street presents Peter Morrison and his guests,   Q20
who introduce the audience to the fine Scottish tradition of
popular singing. This show begins at 8 p.m.

To find out more about events or places to visit, please call at
the Tourist Information Centre at 5, Waverley Bridge, or telephone 226 6591.

We do hope you enjoy your day in the capital, and thank you
for calling.

pause

tone

Now you will hear the piece again.

> **TONE** Rewind the cassette to zero to hear the passage a
> second time.

pause

That is the end of the third part of the test.

pause

Fourth Part

You will hear a conversation between two people who work in a
hospital. For questions 21–23 fill in the information in the gaps
provided.

WHERE THE
CLUES ARE

↓

pause

tone

┌───┐
│ ★TONE★ Set the counter on your cassette player to zero now. │
└───┘

DIARY BOOKING

Wendy: . . . . and, er, what else did she say? Oh, you've got a
        pageful there.
Chris: Oh, all sorts of odds and ends. Er, well another thing I
        wanted to tell you was that the Heart Foundation   Q21
        have booked the assembly hall for Friday the 30th of   Q22
        September (*Hmm*) and they want to borrow a projec-
        tor and screen.   Q23
Wendy: What kind of projector?
Chris: I don't know. He's going to check up on that. He just
        wanted to know whether it would be OK and I said,
        'Well, the security aspect is going to worry us,
        because there's another party in on the Saturday so
        we've got to make sure it's locked up and away on
        that Friday night.' So he's going to get Bill Ainsworth
        to make sure that it's locked up and put away . . .
Wendy: Who's Bill Ainsworth?
Chris: Oh, er, he's the head porter. They have to sit on the
        desk. (*Oh, yeah*) Er, er, the security aspect and all
        that . . . Now, if you could put that in your diary.
Wendy: 30th September?
Chris: 30th September – projector and screen.   Q23
Wendy: Projector and screen – assembly hall. Oh, I'm on   Q22
        holiday!
Chris: Well, you'll have to delegate!
Wendy: Oh, yeah? There's nobody to delegate to . . .
Chris: Um, delegate to Connie, Assistant AVA officer.
Wendy: Oh, ha, ha, ha! Anything else for me?
Chris: Er, no, no, that was all. Um, well, we'd better get
        back. It's 11 o'clock.
Wendy: Oh, yes!

pause

Now you will hear the piece again.

★★TONE★★ Rewind the cassette to zero to hear the passage a
second time.

---

pause

That is the end of the fourth part of this test.

There will now be a pause to allow you to check your work. The
question papers will then be collected by your supervisor.

pause

tone

That is the end of the test.

PART FOUR   The Interview

The FCE Interview format

What happens during the Interview?
The examiner will ask you to come in and sit down. He or she will ask you a few simple questions about yourself, and check your name and candidate number. Then you will be asked to talk about a picture. You may be asked to look at a short written passage, but you will not be asked to read aloud. The passage will be linked to the picture you have looked at in some way, and you may be asked to talk about this. Lastly, the examiner will ask you to take part in some kind of discussion or role play activity.

How long does it last?
The whole Interview will last between 12 and 15 minutes.

Will I take the Interview alone?
You may take the Interview on your own or with another student. This depends on the people who are organizing the timetables at your exam centre. If you have been studying on your own, you will probably take the Interview alone. What happens is the same, but if you are with a friend you will spend more time talking to him or her while the examiner listens to you both.

Using the sample Interview

The purpose of the recorded Interview is to help you understand clearly what will happen and what sort of questions you will be asked.
Note: The materials and questions in *your* Interview will be different. It is no use learning answers by heart.

After you have read this section:

1   Look at the sample Interview materials on pp. 199–201.

2   Load the cassette and find the beginning of the Interview section.

3   Listen carefully to the candidate and see how he takes the opportunity to show the examiner what he can say.
How well does he do, do you think?

4   Look at the Tapescript and read the commentary on the right.

5   Listen again to check your understanding and consider the comments.

Suggestion: If you have a friend who speaks good English and who is willing to help you, let him or her listen to the recorded Interview. This will help him or her to take the examiner's role and give you some practice.

Candidate materials for the Interview

PAPER 5   THE INTERVIEW

<u>Photographs</u>

1

2

3

Passages

1 It's a hard life, but I'm not complaining about
that. I love horses and I love the atmosphere at a
race meeting. Now I want the feeling of my first
winner in this country.

2 Look at those lovely creatures. I bet they're good
milkers. The judges'll have a job picking the
winners, won't they?

3 It's quite simple really — if you love them they'll
love you. A dog's devotion to its master is
absolute. That's why a dog is the best friend a man
can have.

Tasks

1 List of animals

cat	elephant	horse
dog	goat	pig
mouse	cow	rabbit
hen	camel	snake, etc.

You will be asked to select the following and give reasons for your choice:
a) Two animals that are especially useful to man in his work
b) Two animals that are reared for their skins or as food
c) Two animals that would make good pets

2 Discussion

'We should respect animals and not use them for our own purposes. We have no right to sell animals for food, use animals in medical research, or use animals for entertainment.'

3 Discussion

'We are not doing enough to conserve the wildlife of this world.'

Tapescript

Paper 5   The Interview

The sample Interview		*Commentary*
Examiner:	Hello.	
Candidate:	Hello.	
Examiner:	That's your marksheet, is it? Can I take that, please?	*The examiner will begin by checking your name and probably your index number. She will ask for your marksheet (which you will have been given just before you enter the interview room).*
Candidate:	Yes, of course.	
Examiner:	Thank you. And you are Abbas, is that right?	*Then you will probably be asked a little about yourself. This is just to 'break the ice' and help you relax. For example, you should be prepared to explain your job or your studies, to describe your home or family, to say why you are studying English, or to talk about your plans for the future.*
Candidate:	Yes, I am.	
Examiner:	Right, Abbas. Um, what do you do, are you a student or . . .?	
Candidate:	Um, I'm a photographer.	
Examiner:	A photographer *(Yes)* ah, what sort of things do you take photographs of?	
Candidate:	Well, usually, er, still life, and close-up photography.	
Examiner:	So you take pictures of things rather than *(Yes)* people?	
Candidate:	Yes.	
Examiner:	Yes, and, and this is your job?	
Candidate:	That's my job, that's right. *(Yeah)* I do it commercially.	
Examiner:	Aha, yeah. Gosh, it sounds really interesting. *(Thank you)* Now I am going to show you some photographs, I suppose you're used to looking at pictures: I'd like you to look at the first one of these three photographs. Take a few moments, and when you are ready I'd like you to, um, tell me what you can see in the photograph and tell me what you	*Now the Interview is really beginning.*
		See page 199.
		She really means this – don't feel you must begin to speak immediately – give yourself enough time to study the

think about the picture . . . tell me
what you think about it. When
you're ready.

*material thoroughly and
think what you want to say.
Remember, the examiner
wants your ideas about the
picture, not just a list of the
objects on it.*

Candidate: Sorry, did you say the first one?
Examiner: Yeah.

*If you're not absolutely
clear about what you have
to do, ask for clarification.
It's quite all right to do this.
You can also say, for
example:*
   *I'm sorry, would you
mind repeating that?
or*

Candidate: Yes, I think I am ready.
Examiner: Yes, OK.
Candidate: Well, it's a, it's a woman and a dog,
(Mhm) I don't know what sort of dog,
I'm not very good at recognizing the
(No, no) species, but definitely that's
a dog (Yes) and it seems that the
woman is somehow talking to the
dog. (Mhm) Um, I don't think she is
trying to train the dog – it's some sort
of – just, um, talking and touching
her.

   *Please could you say that
again?*

*Of course, you're not
expected to know what sort
of dog! Don't worry if you
can't always find the exact
word for everything in the
picture. It's much better to
say 'touching the dog' for
example, if you can't
remember or don't know
'pat' or 'stroke', than to say
nothing.*

Examiner: Do you think it's her dog?
Candidate: I don't think so. (Ah) It seems that it's
in the park and it's somebody else's
dog, and perhaps this woman's been
walking and noticed this beautiful
dog and just sat there and talked to
her.
Examiner: She likes the dog?
Candidate: Yes, definitely, (Ah) it looks as she's
enjoying just touching her, and
talking to her.
Examiner: Uhuh. So it's quite a friendly
atmosphere, do you think?
Candidate: Yes, definitely.
Examiner: Do you, would you do something
like that, would you . . .?
Candidate: Oh yes, definitely, yes. I like dogs

*This is a good answer. You
should avoid answering
with just 'Yes' or 'No'.
Always try to explain your
opinion. It doesn't matter
what your opinion is,
provided you explain it
properly, using the material
in front of you.*

This is good, because the

and cats *(Mhm)* very much. *(Aha)* I used to be frightened of dogs *(Mhm)* but now I'm not *(Aha, yes)* because I've been here long enough not to be frightened of dogs.

Examiner: Aha, what, do you mean in England, you've got used to having *(Yes)* but you wouldn't have dogs around you much at home?

Candidate: Not really. Not as much as here. *(Mhm)* There are dogs there but they are mainly kept for guards, they're guard dogs. And, of course the, the time I was there, in certain area of the town there were a lot of stray dogs, *(Aha)* and at night they, they attacked people sometimes.

Examiner: So as a child you were nervous?

Candidate: As a child, yes, I was frightened *(Yeah)* and nervous *(Yeah)* of getting very close to the dogs *(Mhm, yeah)* – but they are – we also know that dogs are very nice and they say they are very loyal, *(Mhm)* because as a child, we sometimes fed the dogs in the street, in the narrow lanes *(Mm)* and that was in the evening coming home. And next morning we noticed that the dog's been behind our front door, in the street, all night sitting there, and what we didn't know was that, as a child, that it wasn't because of the loyalty but it was because there was a source of food there perhaps, the dog was sitting there, for us to give *(More food)* more food, yes, but we interpreted it as *(Ah)* it's loyal, *(Yeah)* you give them a bit of food *(Yeah)* and they just sit there, *(Yeah)* and, and wait for you .

Examiner: Well, that's very interesting. I'd like you now to look at a little piece of writing. If you look on the, um, this other page, you'll see three short passages. *(Yes)* I want you to look at the third passage. *(Yes)* Don't read it

candidate is extending the conversation by introducing his own ideas. He's not merely responding to the questions.

See page 200.

Candidate, Examiner dialogue on left; commentary notes on right.

to me. *(Mm)* I'd like you just to read it to yourself and then I'd like you to tell me how you think it is linked to the photograph we've been talking about. Do they have the same theme, do you think? The third passage and the photograph we've been talking about.

Candidate: I don't think so. I can't see anything related in the picture. *(Aha)* There are some cows or cattles.

He misunderstood the instruction, but this is not a serious problem and can soon be put right.

Examiner: Sorry, um the photograph we, you described to me.

Candidate: Oh, I see, I'm sorry, I was . . .

Examiner: And this third passage here.

Candidate: Right, so we're talking about the third passage, to the photograph, the first photograph I saw . . .

He checks that he now understands correctly.

Examiner: That's right, yes.

Candidate: I'm sorry. Yes, OK. *(That's OK)* Can you give me another *(Yes, yes, sure)* second, read it again then, I'm sorry.

It's quite acceptable to ask for extra time if you need it.

Examiner: Yes, of course.

Candidate: Yes, yes, this is directly related to the photograph, *(Mhm)* talking about dog. It's, it's somehow there, there is affection from both dogs to the person and from the person to the dog. *(Mhm)* It's there. I thought it wasn't, that the lady there wasn't the dog's master, but, I mean, that's the only thing which, I think it's not relevant, but that was purely my guess, it could be her master .

The photograph and the passage may not always be so closely related as these. The words may be spoken or written by someone in the photograph, or be about them.

Although you mustn't read all the passage aloud, it can be useful to quote a few words to support your opinion.

There's no 'right' or 'wrong' answer about who the woman is. It's a matter of opinion.

Examiner: But it is about the same thing that you were talking about, isn't it?

Candidate: That's right, the lady is very kind to the dog, you can see it's caressing her or him and, er, *(And the dog)* it's a very friendly atmosphere, and the dog is very friendly, *(Yeah)* very

He means 'she's caressing it'.

	relaxed. *(Mhm)* Is there any more you . . .?	
Examiner:	No, that's, that's um that's very interesting. Now I've got one more thing I want you to do. On this last page *(Yes)* you'll see there's a list of animals *(Yes)* and what I would like you to do is to look at the list and to choose two animals which are useful *(Yes)* to man, two animals which we use, for example, for food, or something like that, *(Yes)* and two animals which we can keep as pets. *(Right)* Tell me which animals you think would be right for each of those. You may not think any of them fit one of those categories.	*See page 201.* *The third part of the Interview may take various forms: it may consist of a role play, you may be asked what you would do in a certain situation, or to give your opinion on a subject. It's important to listen carefully as the examiner explains what you must do.*
Candidate:	So the first category would be, erm, what man uses . . .	*It's always worth checking you have understood the instructions by repeating them.*
Examiner:	Yes, in, in work, for example.	
Candidate:	Right, well, a horse is one of them *(Yeah)* definitely, er dog is another one.	
Examiner:	Aha, how does man use a dog in, for work?	
Candidate:	Well, dogs are very good to be trained for, well, police use them, to start with *(Aha, aha, yeah)* a lot, because they've got very strong sense of smell, and *(Mhm)* by training them, they can, er in several areas, they can make use of a dog, and dog can help.	
Examiner:	Looking for things . . .	
Candidate:	Looking for things, rescuing the people in the mountain, *(Aha, yeah)* or in the 'costum' if, if there are some drugs or anything amongst the . . .	*He mispronounces a word, so his meaning is not very clear.*
Examiner:	Ah, yes, the Customs Officers use them. Yeah, yeah.	*The examiner is checking that she has understood, she's not correcting him, examiners don't do that. He corrects himself – this is a good thing to do if you can.*
Candidate:	Customs Officer, yes, they use them, *(Mhm)* police use them *(Mhm)* definitely, for chasing, not chasing as such, well, sometimes, yes, chasing but for sniffing the criminal's clothes and *(Aha)* that kind of thing *(Yeah)*	

and to trace the person. *(Yeah)* There
are so many other areas *(Yeah)* – in
the farm, they use sheep dog, *(Oh,
yes, yes)* sheep dog, they use it to
look after the sheep *(Aha, aha)* when
they gather them.

Examiner: What about the next, the next part?
The *(The next part)* what about
animals we use for food or for their
skins?

Candidate: Well, cow is one animal we use for
the food, a lot of people like rabbit,
(Mhm) they eat rabbit. Er . . .

Examiner: Mm, something makes me think that
you don't like – the way you said
that.

Candidate: No, I think somehow rabbit are too
innocent to be eaten.

Examiner: Too small *(Too small, yes)* and
cuddly? But you don't mind eating a
cow – because it's bigger, is it?

Candidate: Well, not exactly that, it's – to eat
beef or cow meat is something that –
I, I've been eating meat since I *(Mm)*
remember and beef was one of the
kind of meat *(Mm)* I ate. *(Mm)* And
rabbit wasn't *(Aha)* very common.

Examiner: What about the third category?
(Sorry, what was the) Animals we
keep for pets?

Candidate: Oh, for pet – yes, there are, well,
there are cats, dogs, um, again
rabbit. *(Yeah)* Some people keep
snake as, as pet.

Examiner: Do you think that's a good thing to
do?

*She's probably asking about
snakes.*

Candidate: Oh, I think it is. Keeping pet is very
healthy thing to do. *(Mm)* Um . . .

Examiner: Why?

*He interprets the question
more generally – this doesn't
matter.*

Candidate: Because there is some sort of
relationship between person and,
and a person's er, pet, it's always
one-sided, so you can talk to your pet
and say whatever you want to and
(And your) that pet never disagrees or
anything.

Examiner: Do you, you have a pet yourself, do
                you?
Candidate: I've got a cat.
Examiner: You've got a cat.
Candidate: Yes.
Examiner: And, and what, you talk to that, do
                you?
Candidate: Yes, I think I do sometimes.
Examiner: Yes, I must admit I do the same
                sometimes.
Candidate: Yes, they are very nice. They're very
                nice.
Examiner: You obviously enjoy keeping a cat.
Candidate: Oh, very much, very much so. *(Fine)*
                Yes.
Examiner: Well, that's the end of the interview.
                Thank you very much indeed. *(Thank*
                you) Wasn't too bad, was it?
Candidate: No, it was very good. Thank you.
Examiner: Thank you. Bye-bye.
Candidate: Bye.

The examiner knows that exams aren't fun!

Remember – you must not try to find out how well you have done – the examiner is not allowed to say.

In fact, the candidate speaks very well, with very few errors. An interview like this would probably get full marks.

Acknowledgements

The University of Cambridge Local Examinations Syndicate and the publishers are grateful to the following for permission to reproduce texts and illustrations. It has not been possible to identify sources of all the material used and in such cases the publishers would welcome information from copyright owners.

A. D. Peters & Company Ltd for the extract from *The Realms of Gold* by Margaret Drabble on pp. 21–2; Penguin Books Ltd for the adapted blurb from *Claudius The God* by Robert Graves on p. 25; Hodder & Stoughton Ltd and John Farquharson Ltd for the extract from *Smiley's People* by John le Carré on pp. 39–40; Shire Publications Ltd and Nigel Harvey for the extract from *Discovering Farm Livestock* by Nigel Harvey on p. 41; A. P. Watt Ltd for the extract from *Politics is for People* by Shirley Williams on pp. 77–8; Anchor Hotels for the 'Breakaways' competition on p. 80; Nina Hajnal for the top photo on p. 199; *Cambridge Evening News* for the bottom photo on p. 199; Alger Meekma for the photo on p. 200.

The texts of the Edinburgh Leisureline and Stratford Leisureline are re-recorded and reproduced by kind permission of British Telecom and the Tourist Information Centre, Stratford-on-Avon.

The illustrations on pp. 4, 5 and 6 are by Jeremy Long.

READING COMPREHENSION ANSWER SHEET

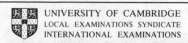 UNIVERSITY OF CAMBRIDGE
LOCAL EXAMINATIONS SYNDICATE
INTERNATIONAL EXAMINATIONS

ENGLISH AS A FOREIGN LANGUAGE

FOR INVIGILATOR'S USE ONLY
Shade here if the candidate
is ABSENT or has WITHDRAWN

↳ ▭

Examination/Paper No.

Examination Title

Centre/Candidate No.

Candidate Name

● Sign here if the above information is correct.

....

● Tell the Invigilator immediately if the information above
is not correct

MULTIPLE-CHOICE ANSWER SHEET

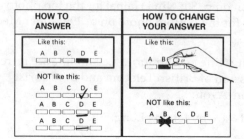

HOW TO ANSWER

Like this:

A B C D E
▭ ▭ ▭ ▬ ▭

NOT like this:

A B C D E
▭ ▭ ▭ ✓ ▭

A B C D E
▭ ▭ ▭ ▭ ▭

A B C D E
▭ ▭ ▭ ▬ ▭

HOW TO CHANGE YOUR ANSWER

Like this:

A B C D E
▬ ▭ ▬ ▭ ▭

NOT like this:

A B C D E
▭ ✗ ▭ ▭ ▭

DO
– use an HB pencil
– rub out any answer
you wish to change

DON'T
– use any other kind of pen
or pencil
– use correcting fluid
– make any marks outside
the boxes

1	A B C D
2	A B C D
3	A B C D
4	A B C D
5	A B C D
6	A B C D
7	A B C D
8	A B C D
9	A B C D
10	A B C D

11	A B C D
12	A B C D
13	A B C D
14	A B C D
15	A B C D
16	A B C D
17	A B C D
18	A B C D
19	A B C D
20	A B C D

21	A B C D
22	A B C D
23	A B C D
24	A B C D
25	A B C D
26	A B C D
27	A B C D
28	A B C D
29	A B C D
30	A B C D

31	A B C D
32	A B C D
33	A B C D
34	A B C D
35	A B C D
36	A B C D
37	A B C D
38	A B C D
39	A B C D
40	A B C D

LISTENING COMPREHENSION ANSWER SHEET

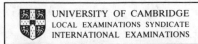

UNIVERSITY OF CAMBRIDGE
LOCAL EXAMINATIONS SYNDICATE
INTERNATIONAL EXAMINATIONS

ENGLISH AS A FOREIGN LANGUAGE

FOR SUPERVISOR'S USE ONLY
Shade here if the candidate
is ABSENT or has WITHDRAWN

Examination/Paper No.

Examination Title

Centre/Candidate No.

Candidate Name

LISTENING COMPREHENSION ANSWER SHEET

TEST NUMBER		FOR OFFICE USE ONLY	[10] [20] [30] [40] [50] [0] [1] [2] [3] [4] [5] [6] [7] [8] [9]

1
2
3
4
5
6
7
8
9
10
11
12
13
14
15
16
17
18
19
20

21
22
23
24
25
26
27
28
29
30
31
32
33
34
35
36
37
38
39
40

41
42
43
44
45
46
47
48
49
50
51
52
53
54
55
56
57
58
59
60

OMR FCE/CPE-4

211

, Lcc.

London Chamber of Commerce

Body Glove
U.S.A.